The Cambridge Manuals of Science and
Literature

THE PEOPLES OF INDIA

Brāhmans
(*Mirzapur district*)

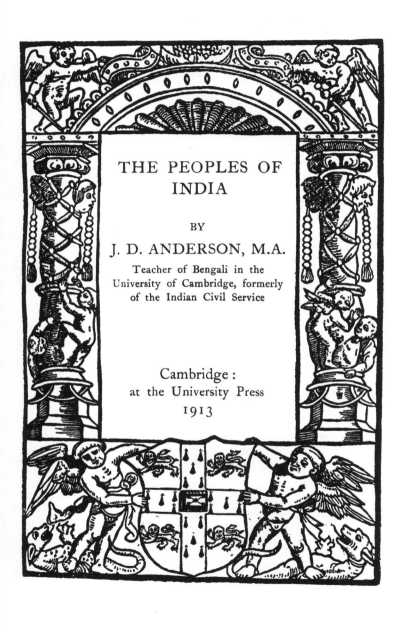

THE PEOPLES OF INDIA

BY

J. D. ANDERSON, M.A.

Teacher of Bengali in the
University of Cambridge, formerly
of the Indian Civil Service

Cambridge:
at the University Press
1913

CAMBRIDGE UNIVERSITY PRESS
Cambridge, New York, Melbourne, Madrid, Cape Town,
Singapore, São Paulo, Delhi, Tokyo, Mexico City

Cambridge University Press
The Edinburgh Building, Cambridge CB2 8RU, UK

Published in the United States of America by
Cambridge University Press, New York

www.cambridge.org
Information on this title: www.cambridge.org/9781107401624

© Cambridge University Press 1913

First published 1913
First paperback edition 2011

A catalogue record for this publication is available from the British Library

ISBN 978-1-107-40162-4 Paperback

*With the exception of the coat of arms
at the foot, the design on the title page is a
reproduction of one used by the earliest known
Cambridge printer, John Siberch, 1521*

PREFACE

THE writing of this little book has been delayed by the hope I once cherished of incorporating in it some of the results of the Indian Census of 1911. This desire was inevitable in the case of a retired Indian official, who, like most of his kind, has taken a small part in one or more of the decennial numberings of the Indian people. In this country, a Census affords material chiefly for the calculations and theories of the statistician, and the Registrar-General is not regarded as an expert in Anthropology or Linguistics. But in India the case is very different. If the district officer is always glad to learn as much as possible of, the people with whom he is brought into contact, his official duties often reveal only the seamy side of Indian life, and it is only when he is in camp, or snatching a rare and hurried holiday in shooting, that he gets to see something of the people otherwise than as litigants or payers of revenue. A census is an agreeable and welcome opportunity for looking at India from another and more genially human point of view. In the first place, it is one of the least

expensive of official operations, since it is chiefly
performed by unpaid and volunteer agency. Hence
the official, a little weary of litigants, touts, pleaders,
and subordinates, who, however amiable in their
private lives, are apt to be indolent and obstructive
in office, is glad to make acquaintance with new
friends, who, for the most part, take an intelligent
and amused interest in the unfamiliar task of numbering. For many busy weeks before the actual counting
takes place, the district officer has to ride far and
near, to satisfy himself that all necessary preparations
have duly been made, to issue the instructions that
may be called for by the zeal, inquisitiveness or
density of his volunteer colleagues. In the process,
he has many pleasant and some amusing experiences.
On one occasion I rode into a little village on the
north-eastern frontier, inhabited by semi-savage
Tibeto-Burmese people. Official orders as to the
numbering of all the house in legible figures had
apparently not been obeyed. I simulated wrath and
disappointment, but the worthy headman on whom
I vented my (purely official) indignation was not
dismayed. "Bring out your drums!" he shouted.
Every householder produced the family kettle-drum,
on the head of which the number of his house had
been duly inscribed in large figures. There was no
paper in the village, but parchment was invented

before paper, and the headman deserved the commendation I was glad to bestow. On another occasion, I found a house numbered indeed, but grievously dilapidated and obviously deserted. "Why is this empty house numbered?" I asked. "It is haunted by a ghost, sir," answered the enumerator. I confess I felt sorry not to allow him to include this ghostly visitant in a census of living men. Other incidents, more ethnologically important than these, will frequently occur. In any case the Census Report of an Indian province is by far the most interesting official document in existence, and each census adds something to our knowledge of Indian humanity, if only because each Census Commissioner, always an officer of unusual ability and attainments, looks at his task from a point of view somewhat different from that of his predecessors, and stamps his individuality on the work of his subordinates. Those who have read Mr E. A. Gait's article on *Caste* in the *Dictionary of Ethics and Religion* will expect the census of 1911 to contain new views and fresh information as to the actual working of the caste system .in various provinces, and its relation to the religious ideas of the people.

It was natural, then, that I should wish to learn from a new tapping of the source from which has

been compiled, for the most part, the ethnical portion
of the first volume of the Imperial Gazetteer of India,
which has been my chief authority in compiling this
little book. But I know not when Mr Gait's Report
for all India will be ready, and even the Provincial
Reports come but slowly from the Press. Most of
them are full of the most interesting and valuable
information, but it takes time to assimilate so much
new matter, and, in any case, not much of it could
have been utilized for so small and elementary a
book. Hence I have simply to state my debt to the
late Sir H. H. Risley and Mr E. A. Gait for the
chapter on Race and Caste ; to Sir G. A. Grierson
for the chapter on Languages, and to Mr William
Crooke for enabling me further to summarise his
masterly summary of what is known about Indian
Religions. It is a particular pleasure to acknowledge
my indebtedness to my friend Sir G. A. Grierson.
Years ago, when we were young men, it was known
that in him the Indian Civil Service possessed a
scholar and a linguist of most unusual industry and
ability. But few knew that there was germinating in
his mind the scheme for the great *Linguistic Survey
of India*, the most remarkable feat of administrative
scholarship, perhaps, that has ever been attempted, a
feat that has won him the *Prix Volney* and I know
not what other appreciations of his work in France

and Germany. His learning and linguistic skill are widely known, but I must seize the opportunity to tell of another feature of his achievement. Of course no man knows more than a few of the hundreds of Indian languages, but there is one man who knows something of the working and mechanism of them all, and that is Sir G. A. Grierson. I had the privilege of helping him with part of the Bodo volume of his *Survey*, having had occasion to learn one or two Tibeto-Burman languages in the course of official duty. The practised ease with which he acquired the syntactical and phonetic peculiarities of languages with which he had no previous acquaintance was the most surprising and delightful intellectual performance I have ever witnessed.

I have ventured occasionally to enliven my chiefly borrowed narrative with personal ideas or reminiscences. Such digressions have however been few and brief, and I do not think I need apologise for them.

I have to thank Miss Lilian Whitehouse and my son, Lieut. M. A. Anderson, R.E., for the two diagrammatic maps which will, I hope, clear up any geographical difficulties created by a necessarily brief account of a large and complicated subject.

I owe the illustrations of caste types to the kindness of Mr William Crooke. They are from photographs of inhabitants of one single district of the United Provinces and are interesting as showing how in a single small area racial differences show themselves in such a way as to be recognisable by the most careless observer. They prove once more how stratified Indian humanity has become under the influence of caste rules of marriages.

J. D. A.

September, 1913.

CONTENTS

ILLUSTRATIONS

MAPS

INTRODUCTION

IT is necessary, once more, to remind the reader that the peninsula of India has an area and population roughly equal to the area and population of Europe without Russia. Everyone who has learnt geography at school is familiar with the great triangle, its base in the soaring Himalayan heights in the north, its apex jutting into the Indian Ocean, and marked by the satellite island of Ceylon. To the north, then, is the great mountain barrier, a tangled mass of snowy peaks, glaciers and snowfields, separating the sunny plains of India proper from the plateaux of Central Asia. Beneath them lie wide river basins, sandy and dry as unirrigated Egypt to the west; moist, warm, and waterlogged to the east. To the south of the valleys of the Indus and the Ganges is the central plateau, home of many aboriginal races. This rises on the west into a castellated rampart of hills facing the Arabian Sea, and on the south slopes away into green undulating uplands. So much, at least, of geographical description must be given as a clue to the distribution of the peoples of India.

Along the Himalayas, growing stronger in numbers as we go eastwards, are races mostly of a Mongolian type, mingled with purely Indian elements. In the Panjāb and the United Provinces, sending offshoots southwards along the well-watered west coast, are the peoples in whom the traces of Aryan immigration are most visible. In Bengal we find a duskier race, provisionally termed Mongolo-Dravidian, but with a strong infusion, in the upper classes, of western blood. In the south are a still darker population almost wholly Dravidian. It is in the most ancient part of India, in the high plateau of the Deccan, that there still dwell the peoples who are probably the aborigines of the land and use the most purely Indian languages, the various Dravidian dialects. The geologically recent valleys of the Indus and Ganges are the home of races, mingled with aboriginal peoples, whose language and physical features show that in them is a strong strain of immigrant blood.

On the Himalayan slopes, in Assam, and especially in Burma, are Tibeto-Burman peoples, with something of a Japanese aspect. Intermingled with all these, in forests and on rough and hardly accessible hills, are scattered many groups of semi-savage folk, of whom little was known till the gradual spread of British rule carried the administrator, the missionary, and finally the anthropologist, into regions once considered unfit for the presence of civilised men.

So far, it may be said, the distribution of Indian humanity is not very unlike that of the races of Europe. Even this very crude summary, it is true, shows at least three great groups of languages, Dravidian in the south, Indo-European in the west and north-west, Tibeto-Burman in the north and the north-east. There are in fact five separate families of human speech which have their homes in India; the Aryan, the Dravidian, the Mundā, the Mon-Khmer, and the Tibeto-Chinese. The lateral spread of these is, of course, no real indication of the present habitat of five different races of men. But they do indicate the existence, in varying degrees of purity, of five different origins, of which the Dravidian and Mundā alone can be said to be purely indigenous and confined to the Indian peninsula. Nowhere is it more easy than in India to see how languages spread from race to race, from tribe to tribe, with a sort of linguistic contagion; the stronger, more supple, more copious, more cultivated languages replacing and gradually destroying weaker forms of speech. Something of the same sort has occurred, and is even now happening, in Europe. But the surviving European languages are mostly sturdy and vigorous, and do not readily yield place to one another. In India the process of linguistic invasion is going on before our eyes, attendant on the gradual growth of Hindu civilisation and religion, which

1—2

disdains to practise open and reasoned proselytism, but extends its borders nevertheless, and carries with it one or another of the Aryan dialects.

In spite of the spread of the stronger languages, the five great families of Indian speech remain and testify to more varied origins than those of Europe. One of the first results of familiarity with Indian peoples is a sense of their remarkable variety of aspect and culture. When the stranger lands in India, his first feeling is one of bewildering sameness; the dusky beings that surround him seem as like one another as sheep, or peas. But that sensation is merely due to the predominance of unfamiliar colour, and soon gives way to an impression of astonishing and most interesting variety. This variety is exhibited by the careful anthropometric investigations of the ethnologist. But there is more variety than average measurements show, and the rough impressions of the experienced administrator and traveller are not without their value. For instance, Sir William Hunter, in his work on *The Indian Empire*, classified the highlanders of Chota Nagpore as a race apart, whom he called Kolārians. Sir H. H. Risley says that "the distinction between Kolārians and Dravidians is purely linguistic, and does not correspond to any differences of physical type." As a matter of average physical measurements, this criticism is just. The average dimensions of Sonthal skulls are the same as those of other Dravidian races. But he would be a poor observer of racial characteristics, who could not pick out a typical inhabitant of Chota Nagpore from a crowd of southern Dravidians. Even in parts of Bengal where such "Kolārian" folk have settled some generations ago, and have acquired the local language and dress, they are almost as easily distinguished as a Hindu undergraduate in Cambridge. If physical characters are rightly divided into "indefinite" signs of race, which can only be described with difficulty and hesitation in ordinary language, and the "definite" signs which can be measured and reduced to figures, yet the general aspect of a tribe or caste is the first thing which strikes an experienced enquirer's eye, and leads him to make further and more detailed investigations.

So is it also with those divisions, peculiar to India, which are known to us by the Portuguese name of *caste*. The Indian name for caste is *varna*, or "colour," and physical differences between different castes were fairly obvious even before accurate averages were struck between many individual measurements. Caste has undoubtedly tended, and for similar reasons, to perpetuate such differences between classes of men as we readily recognise between different breeds of horses or cattle. The ages of men succeed one another more slowly than the generations of domestic animals, and segregation, in

spite of caste rules, has probably at no time been so
rigid as in the case of pure-bred animals.   But there
is a restriction in the matter of marriage which has
been more or less efficacious, and especially so in the
case of the higher castes, where the women are more
carefully guarded, and pride of birth influences the
future mothers of the race.   In some rare instances,
castes are still racial, preserved from immixture by
much the same feeling which leads the white American
to protect his race from a mingling of Negro or Red
Indian blood.   Other castes are still recognisably the
result and record of such forbidden mixtures.   Sometimes the resulting difference is so great as to be
visible in actual measurements.   Often the result is
a mere peculiarity of aspect, such as enables an
expert to identify a mongrel or a crossbreed among
domesticated animals.   In any case, once a caste is
formed, it is fenced in by matrimonial rules, strict in
proportion to the social status and consideration of
the group.   Not only, then, are the racial origins of
modern India more various than those of Europe, but
such varieties of colour, stature, and culture as exist
tend to be perpetuated.

It has been said, somewhat paradoxically, that
whereas in Europe the divisions between races of
men cut perpendicularly, as it were, so as to be more
or less local and geographical, in India the separating
lines run horizontally, and represent social strata

This, of course, is only partly true. The ancient Hindu theory of caste assumes the existence of four great divisions of Hindu humanity, extending all over India ; namely, Brāhmans or priests, Kshatriyas, or warriors ; Vaiçyas, or trading and professional folk ; and Sūdras, who are most justly and aptly to be described as "the remainder." In all parts of Hindu India may be found representatives of this ancient and theoretical division of humanity, the first two usually claiming a western origin as eagerly as some of us claim a tincture of Norman blood. But it would be incorrect to say that even the highest and purest of these four divisions is of uniform race, or anything approaching to it, all over India. A Bengali Brāhman, for instance, can be more or less easily distinguished from other Bengalis, if he has the typical appearance of his caste. But he is even more easily distinguished from Brāhmans of other Provinces. How much of this last difference is due to mixture of blood, how much to difference of food and climate, it is, of course, difficult to say. But certainly caste produces a difference of breed in addition to the ethnical varieties of origin which differentiate the Indian populations from those of Europe.

Thirdly, some clue to Indian racial differences may be found in the religions of the peninsula. The greatest of these is still the Indian religion *par excellence*, the wonderful collection of varied speculations, beliefs, and practices known to us as Hinduism, and its daughter, the religion of Buddha. The latter has spread far and wide, has subjugated Ceylon and Burma, and is the leading religion of the Far East. At one time, it was supposed to be entirely or nearly extinct in India, although students had discovered traces of its influence in the Vishnuvite sects of Hinduism. Recent researches have shown that an almost unaltered form of Buddhism survives in the very bosom of Hinduism, and is practised under Hindu names among certain castes of Bengal and Orissa. It is to be noted that the investigations into these survivals have been for the most part conducted by Bengali Hindus, among whom is springing up a school of ethnologists and comparative linguists, who only need a better knowledge and understanding of European methods to be invaluable aids to western research in such matters. In Bengal, a work of purely anthropological interest has actually been published in the vernacular, an interesting account of the Chakmas, a Tibeto-Burman but partly Hindu-ised race on the eastern border of Bengal. Closely akin to the lower forms of Hinduism, and often subtly blending with them, are many Animistic religions, most of them professed by aboriginal tribes, speaking *one or other of the aboriginal languages.*

Islam and Christianity are, of course, imported and proselytising religions, and yield few if any clues to racial or social origins. Many Muhammadans profess to be, and not a few are, of authentic foreign origin. But during the seven hundred years of Muslim rule in India, there was much intermarriage with native races, and even more conversion. It is curious that, as in the case of Christianity, the conversions have been mostly among tribes and classes of the humbler sort. These were not denied admission into Hinduism, but they were only admitted on terms of social and racial degradation. Islam and Christianity alike claim to overlook the accidents of birth and status, and hence attract those to whom Hinduism only offered a place among the lowest ranks of its social hierarchy. But even in the case of the religions of Christ and Muhammad, the inveterate Indian tendency to recognise and insist on breed and social status has asserted itself again and again. Among Muhammadans, the Arabic tribal names have come to be the designations of social units which differ but little from the endogamous castes of Hinduism, and the same tendency is already evident among Christian converts. There is a marked reluctance in some quarters among ex-Hindus to intermarry with ex-Muslims, or even to participate in sacramental Communion with them.

As with caste, so with religion, the divisions are not strictly horizontal. As Christianity is not one thing all over Europe, but has differences of creed, ritual, and practice corresponding to racial differences,

so the Hinduism, and even the Muhammadanism, of
different provinces varies.   There is no sharp boundary ; there are elements in common wherever we go.
But just as Dravidian temple architecture can be
easily distinguished, even by the unpractised eye,
from that of the edifices of the Gangetic plains, so
local peculiarities of belief or ritual may come to the
aid of the anthropologist, and may suggest or confirm
distinctions more easily verified and more capable of
scientific proof.

The study of all these matters is not without a
practical and administrative interest at the present
time.   A hundred and fifty years ago, to the racial,
tribal, and caste differences, accompanied by differences of language and religion, were added political
divisions, accentuated by frequent dynastic or predatory wars.   British rule has introduced two power-
ful unifying influences.   Our system of administration,
while it is adapted more or less effectively (more in
some cases, less in others, according to the talent and
character of local officers) to local precedents and
local needs, is moulded by the great supervising
and consolidating authority of the Governor-General
in Council.

Secondly, higher education in India is conducted
for the most part in English, and educated India,
rapidly growing in numbers, has English for its
second language, and is modifying local beliefs,

usages, aspirations, patriotisms in accordance with
ideas more or less consciously assimilated from European teachers and models. No one can deny that
this new unity of India is the direct result of central-
ised British rule. In the far distance of time, all or
nearly all India would, for a while, accept the domina-
tion of some Hindu ruler or dynasty. Under the
Muhammadans, similarly, there were times when the
Emperor at Delhi was the ruler of all or nearly all
India. Under British rule, a much wider and more
populous India, ranging from Baluchistan to Burma,
and only excepting the semi-independent states which
have been allowed to retain sovereign powers, is really
and for the first time part of the greatest administration on earth except that of China, if we look to
numbers. It is a result, as the history of British India
shows, for which we cannot claim the whole credit.
The direction of the great work of unification has
been in British hands ; it has chiefly been carried
out by indigenous agency, and, in matters of detail,
in deference to Indian ideas and Indian suggestions.
Even fifty years ago, few Indians supposed that the
wide Empire of India could be governed save under
British guidance, or without the aid of British bayonets.
The old habitual forces of disruption were too obvious ;
the distrust of one race for another was still too
keenly felt to allow Indian politicians to imagine
a united India under indigenous rule. But as the

educated classes grow in power, in numbers, in self-
reliance, and reliance on one another ; as some of
them are promoted to posts of higher trust and
authority in India, and even in England, it is perhaps
only natural that Indians should suppose that, so far
as politics and administration are concerned, the old
divisions and dissensions are obsolete, and that united
India can in future be governed by native agency.
That is not a matter with which ethnology has anything to do.   It is the ethnologist's business merely
to record impartially what racial, tribal, social, and
religious differences still survive, and, if he can, to
show how far they have been, and are being, ob-
literated by the spread of education, and by growing
self-confidence and ambition among educated Indians.
Whether the information the ethnologist collects can
be put to any administrative use does not concern
him, nor does he desire that his impartiality shall be
affected by these considerations.   But, in a little book
of this kind it may not be amiss to point out that one
result of British rule has been the growth of a new
type of Indian, the educated Indian ; who, whether he
be Hindu or Muhammadan or Buddhist, is at least
inclined to subordinate the old hereditary divisions
to common political ambitions.   These ambitions
affect the fortunes and the future of some three
hundred millions of humbler Indians, at present only
linked by the accident of common British rule, and,

Plate I

Mahābrāhmans
(*Mirzapur district*)

so far as they are Hindus, by a common Hindu
sentiment.

In the following chapters, it will be my business
to tell, as briefly and clearly as possible, of (1) the
Ethnology and Castes of the Indian Peoples; (2) the
Languages of India; (3) the Religions of India. I hope
what I have already said will sufficiently show why
these three subjects are treated in this order.

CHAPTER I

RACE AND CASTE

CURIOUSLY enough, the systematic enquiry into
the physical race-characteristics of the Indian peoples
was due to a daring assertion by Mr Nesfield, of the
Indian Educational Service, to the effect that, so far
as physical signs go, there is practically only one
Indian race and one Indian caste. This was a hasty
but quite natural generalisation from experience of
a part of India, the United Provinces, which is in the
heart of the Aryan settlement in the Gangetic *do-āb*
(the area between "two rivers"). Here caste has
long been a settled institution, and innumerable sub-
castes, professional or the result of outcasting, have
come into existence. Mr Nesfield was driven by his
local observations to assert the unity of one great

Indian race ; he denied the truth of "the modern
doctrine which divides the population of India into
Aryan and aboriginal": he sturdily declared that it
was impossible to distinguish a scavenger from a
Brāhman, save by costume and other artificial and
accidental marks.   Even in the United Provinces
this uncompromising statement awoke dissent.   In
other parts of India, as, for instance, on the north-
eastern frontier, the crowded home of many races
and languages, dissent was eager and loud.   It was
evident, on the face of it, that Mr Nesfield's new
dogma was based on too limited a study.   Caste, for
him, was a mere matter of hereditary function and
profession; since most castes in the sacred "midland"
of Hinduism have assumed that guise.   There is no
reason to suppose that castes have usually or even
often been formed as professional guilds.   They come
into being for many reasons, some of which will be
presently stated; and in civilised communities, where
the division of labour and specialisation of professional skill are well established, a caste gradually
assumes some distinctive means of livelihood.   But
on the borders of Hinduism, where the Hindu social
system is still assimilating new races, instances abound
of racial castes, tribal castes, perhaps even (though
this is a more doubtful matter) totemistic castes.

Those who had the widest experience of the
Peninsula were convinced that its races were at

least as varied as those of Europe: those who, like Mr Nesfield, had made a close study of one limited tract, might have continued to believe that under the superficial distinctions of caste and class lay a real unity of race. But Mr (afterwards Sir H. H.) Risley had spent the early years of his Indian service among the Dravidian tribes of Chota Nagpore, and was aware that they differ more widely from the people Mr Nesfield had studied than an Englishman differs from a Turk. The difference, indeed, was almost as great as that between a European and a Chinaman. Could such differences be registered and described in such a way as to convince minds accustomed to scientific accuracy in statement? Mr Risley thought he saw his way to an ethnological classification of Indian races and castes by means of the then comparatively new methods of anthropometry. In 1891, he published in the *Journal of the Anthropological Institute* a paper which marked the beginning of systematic ethnological studies in India. It contained a summary of the measurements of eightynine castes and tribes of Bengal, the United Provinces, and Bihār. It dealt, therefore, with the great alluvial plain, created by the Ganges and Indus, which lies between the Himalayas and the *massif central* of the Deccan. Here is the home of the Aryan immigrants, where the great Indo-European languages are spoken by communities as numerous as the larger European nations. Anthropometry showed in the plainest, the most incontrovertible way, that the caste system of marriages had sorted out men into classes possessing definite and recognisable physical characteristics. There were local differences, and caste differences. It only remained to extend anthropometrical measurements to other parts of India to prove that the many languages and religious beliefs of India are associated with an even greater variety of physical qualities. Such enquiries are still in progress, but many notable results have already been obtained, especially by Mr Edgar Thurston, in his now famous investigations into Dravidian ethnography.

The most important and significant measurement is that of the shape of the head. It is, of course, impossible to take a man at random and to say with certainty that the excessive length or breadth of his skull proves him to belong to a given race. But the average skull-measurements of a race are distinctive, and confirm, on the whole, the impressions created by general aspect, colour, language and other vaguer indications. The general result is as follows. At either end of the Himalayan range, in Baluchistan on the west, and in Assam and Burma on the east, broad heads prevail. Broad too are the heads of the mostly Mongolian races inhabiting the valleys of the southern slopes of the Himalayas, and in a belt of

country running down the western coast at least as
far south as Coorg. In the Panjāb, Rājputānā, and
the United Provinces, tracts where the climate is dry
and healthy, where great summer heat is compensated
for by a bracing winter, where wheat is for the most
part the staple food, long heads predominate. In
Bihār, travelling eastwards, medium heads are most
common. In the damp and steamy delta of Bengal,
inhabited by over forty millions of rather dusky rice-
eating people, there is a marked tendency towards
the Mongolian brachy-cephaly of Tibeto-Burman
races. It is visible among the Muhammadans and
Chandāls of Eastern Bengal, people who are probably
indigenous in this tract, it is more marked among the
Kāyasthas, the writer-caste of Bengal, which claims
a western and Aryan origin. It reaches its maximum
development among the Bengali Brāhmans. South
of the Vindhya mountains, where the population is
chiefly Dravidian, with a comparatively small and
ancient mixture of northern blood, the prevalent
type is mainly long-headed or medium-headed. The
coast-population has been much affected by foreign
influences. On the east coast Malayan, Indo-Chinese
and even Portuguese settlers have altered the local
type. On the west coast, Arab, Persian, African,
European, and Jewish immigrants have mingled with
local races, and have changed their physiognomy,
stature, and character of mind and body.

It is still a moot point, which the Mendelists may some day settle for us, whether head-form is a true hereditary race-characteristic, whether the osseous structure of the body generally is not a result of climate, food and other such circumstances of environment. Yet the shape of the head as shown by average measurements does mark off races of men which are separated by other differences than those of habitat. They do correspond to those vaguer yet unmistakeable characteristics which enable us to tell one race from another. The Mongolian, even when he settles in the plains of Assam, Bengal, or Burma and takes to a diet of rice and fish, keeps his round head and his smooth hairless face. The Aryan of the north-west has a markedly long head, which, in his case, goes with a fair complexion and luxuriant beard. The Dravidian, darkest of Indian races, with a tendency to crinkly or curly hair, has also a long or medium head. The mixed races of Bengal have, it is not surprising to find, medium heads, which tend in the upper castes to become broad.

Another significant index to race is the measurement of the nose. The results of nose-measurements roughly divide the peoples of India into three classes —those having narrow or fine noses (leptorrhine), in which the width is less than 70 per cent. of the height; those having medium noses (mesorrhine), with an average index of from 70 to 85; and broad-nosed

(platyrrhine) people, the width of whose noses exceed
85 per cent.   Here we get a physical means of distinguishing between the long-headed people of north-
western India, fair and stalwart, and the almost
equally long-headed dusky folk of the south.   For
the average nose of southern India, in Madras, the
Central Provinces, and Chota Nagpore, is broad.   In
the Panjáb and Baluchistan we get fine noses of what,
to us Europeans, seems an aristocratic type.   In
Afghanistan, noses are so long and hooked as to give
the tall and vigorous Afghan a Jewish aspect.   In the
rest of India, and especially down the west coast,
noses are of medium type.   A still more interesting
discovery is the fact that anywhere outside the Aryan
tracts of the north-west, the broad nose is a distinct
sign of aboriginal blood.   In Bengal, for instance, the
lower castes have broad noses.   The priestly and
writer castes, for all their broad heads, have fine
noses, which support their claim to a western origin.
Roughly speaking, the broad nose goes with primitive
forms of social organisation, with totemistic exogamous clans.   Finer noses are usually associated with
communities of a more modern type; and above these
again come social units, castes and tribes, which claim
descent from eponymous saints and heroes.

   A third physical measurement enables us to effect
a further sorting out of Indian races.   What is called
the "flatness" of the Mongolian face is plain to the

                                                    2   2

most careless observer. This is due chiefly to the formation of the cheekbone, and its relation to the socket of the eye and the root of the nose. This can be measured and expressed in figures, with the result that the Mongoloid people of the north-east and the Himalayan region can be definitely distinguished from the broad-headed races of Baluchistan, Bombay, and Coorg.

Finally, it is possible to arrive at the average stature of various Indian races and communities. The tallest races are found in the north-west, in Baluchistan, the Panjāb and Rājputānā. A progressive diminution is seen as we go down the valley of the Ganges, until we find very short folk among the Assam hill tribes. The Dravidians of the south are shorter than the Aryans of the north. The smallest Indian tribe is that of the Negritos of the Andaman Islands, whose average height is only 4 feet 10½ inches.

From a careful comparison of these measurements, Sir Herbert Risley arrived at the classification of Indian humanity, which, for the moment, is the accepted division, into seven main physical types. Beginning with the north-western frontier, these are as follows:—

(1) The *Turko-Iranian* type, which comprises the Baloches, Brāhuis and Afghans of Baluchistan and the north-west Frontier Province. These are

probably the result of a fusion of Turkī and Persian blood, and are all Muhammadans. The general aspect is wholly different from that of other Indian races, and no one who has ever seen an Afghan or Baloch, with his long Jewish nose and plentiful hair and beard, can ever confuse this type with any other. In temperament also these men of the border differ from other Indians. They are a fierce and warlike race, engaged in constant blood-feuds with one another.

(2)   The *Indo-Aryan* type, with its home in the Panjāb, Rājputānā and Kashmir, has as its most conspicuous members the Rājputs, Khattris and Jāts. These, in all but colour (and even in colour they are hardly more dusky than the races round the Mediterranean) closely resemble the well-bred European in type. In stature they are tall, their complexion is fair; "eyes dark; hair on face plentiful; head long; nose narrow and prominent, but not specially long." One significant peculiarity of this group is that there is little difference in physical character between the upper and lower classes. This, as we shall presently see, is what we should expect from what is known of the history of these peoples. The upper social ranks probably represent the blood, but little diluted with indigenous mixture, of the Aryan immigrants. Even in the lower classes, the typical Aryan characteristics are now so prominent that any indigenous strain that

exists is no longer noticeable in average measurements. Only in height, a quality especially sensitive to differences of food and sanitation, are the lower castes inferior. Here we get a remarkable modern instance of transformation of type. The preaching of the Sikh reformers, involving a change of food and the inculcation of martial discipline and fervour, has converted the despised scavenging Chuhrā into the soldierly Mazhabi, once a redoubtable foe of the English, and now one of the finest soldiers in the British army.

(3) The *Scytho-Dravidian* type, including the Marāthā Brāhmans, the Kunbīs, and the Coorgs of western India. These peoples differ from the Turko-Iranian races in being shorter, in having longer heads, higher noses, and flatter faces.

(4) The *Aryo-Dravidian* or Hindostāni type, which exists in the United Provinces, in parts of Rājputānā, and in Bihār. This type appears to be due to a mixture of Indo-Aryan and Dravidian strains. The higher classes resemble Indo-Aryans, the lower have a distinctly Dravidian aspect. Yet, even to the eye, they form a type apart and are easily recognised. In this type, the average nose-index corresponds exactly to social status. The noses grow broader as we go downwards in the social scale.

(5) The very interesting *Mongolo-Dravidian* or *Bengali* type which is found in Bengal and Orissa.

Here Aryan influences may still be detected in the
upper classes, but there has been extensive mingling
with Tibeto-Burman and Dravidian peoples, and other
aboriginal inhabitants.   The main distinguishing
feature is the broad head, which is most conspicuous
in the upper classes.   It is shared equally by the
Bengali Brāhman, who claims a western origin, and
the Chittagong Mag, whose Tibeto-Burman origin
is not denied.   The Brāhman, on the other hand,
inherits a fine and narrow nose, which may very well
be due to Indo-Aryan ancestry.   Recent investigations tend to show that Buddhism survived till a
comparatively recent date in Bengal.   Hence, no
doubt, a temporary disregard of caste restrictions
and a freer mixture with local strains.

   (6)   The *Mongoloid* type of the Himalayas, Nepāl,
Assam, and Burma.   "The head is broad: complexion
dark, with a yellowish tinge ; hair on face scanty ;
stature short or below average ; nose fine to broad ;
face characteristically flat ; eyelids often oblique."
Here we have races which, if somewhat dark, correspond to the ideas most of us entertain about the
external aspect and temperament of the Siamese or
Japanese.   In intellectual ability, and what we may
call the artistic faculty, they are inferior to the
Bengali.   Most Europeans, however (or is it, therefore ?) find them among the most congenial of Indian
races.   They are social, good-natured, straightforward

people. In the western Himalayas, there has been intermixture with Aryan invaders, as in the Kangra Valley and Nepāl, and the ruling dynasties claim Rājput origin, for the Indo-Aryans loved to settle in the cool hills, much as the Anglo-Indian does to this day. But on the mountainous frontiers of North-East Bengal and Assam, the Mongoloid peoples have remained undisturbed till our own time. Linguistically, this group is peculiarly interesting, since they speak many tongues, many of which still remain to be recorded and studied by European scholars.

(7) The *Dravidian* type, which extends from Ceylon to the valley of the Ganges and covers all South-Eastern India. It is found in Madras, Hyderabad, the Central Provinces, most of Central India, and Chota Nagpore. Its purest representatives dwell on the Malabar coast and in Chota Nagpore. Here we have probably the original inhabitants of India, now modified in some degree by an infiltration of Aryan, Scythian and Mongoloid elements. "The stature is short or below mean; the complexion very dark, approaching black; hair plentiful, with an occasional tendency to curl; eyes dark; head long; nose very broad, sometimes depressed at the root, but not so as to make the face appear flat."

It must, of course, be understood, that these types and the names allotted to them merely show that in certain areas the average characteristics of the peoples

Plate II

Kāyasthas—the writer caste
(*Mirzapur district*)

dwelling there can be sufficiently separated to be
recognisable not only by eye but by the callipers of
the anthropologist.   The names, it will be noticed,
in some cases, imply theories as to the origin of the
races thus grouped together.   These theories are
partly based on measurements, partly on tradition,
partly on linguistic considerations.   It remains for
me to state, very rapidly, what these theories are.

That the Dravidians are the oldest race in India
is rendered *primâ facie* probable by the fact that
they inhabit the southernmost part of the peninsula,
between races who can with some certainty be called
invaders—and the deep sea.   There is a remarkable
uniformity of physical characteristics among the lower
specimens of this type.   They have in common an
animistic religion, their distinctive language, their
peculiar stone monuments, and a primitive system
of totemism.   They do not resemble Europeans on
the one hand, or the races of the Far East on the
other.   Until proof to the contrary is forthcoming
they may well be regarded as the autochthones of
India.

There is more room for difference of opinion as to
the origins of the brilliant and highly civilised Indo-
Aryans of the Panjāb and Rājputānā.   As I have said
before, we have here a population closely resembling
that of modern Europe in many respects.   I might
have added that it still more closely resembles the

Europe of the Roman empire. Nowhere else in
Hindu India does caste sit so lightly, or approach
so nearly to the social classes of Europe. Though
there are rules, or rather customs, forbidding intermarriage between different castes, yet these are
mitigated by the custom, not unknown to ourselves,
of *hypergamy*. This simply means that a man may
take a wife from a lower caste, but will not give his
daughters to men of that caste. The result is a
uniformity of physical type found nowhere else in
India. Moreover these people speak a language of
the Indo-European family, and have many words and
idioms in common with ourselves. The present theory
of their origin is simply that they are in the bulk
immigrants into India, immigrants who came into
the land from the north-west with their herds and
families, as the Jews entered into and possessed
Palestine.

One chief objection to this theory is that the
lands through which they must have passed are in
no way fitted to be an *officina gentium*, being now
dry, barren, and all but deserted. But abundant
indications remain to show that the climate of South-
Eastern Persia and the tracts to the north has
changed within comparatively recent times. The
relics of crowded populations and ancient civilisa-
tions abound in regions now sandy desert, and there
is evidence in the tales told by Greek and Chinese

travellers that the Panjāb itself, most of it comparatively arid, was once well wooded. The theory
then is that the homogeneous and handsome population of the Panjāb and Rājputānā represents the
almost pure descendants of Aryan settlers, who
carried the Indo-European languages now prevailing
over Northern India, just as our own emigrants took
the English language to America.

But we have also to account for the Aryo-
Dravidians who inhabit the sacred "midland" country
of Hinduism, and here we have Dr Hoernle's now
famous theory, remarkably confirmed by the researches of Sir George Grierson's *Linguistic Survey*.
This theory supposes that a second swarm of Aryan-
speaking people, perhaps driven forward by the
change of climate in central Asia, entered India
through the high and difficult passes of Gilgit and
Chitral, and established themselves in the fertile
plains between the Ganges and the Jumna. They
followed a route which made it impossible for their
women to accompany them. They took to themselves
wives from the daughters of dusky Dravidian aborigines. Here, by contact with a different, and in
their sentiment, inferior race, caste came into being.
Here most of the Vedic hymns were composed. Here,
by a blending of imported and indigenous religious
ideals, the ritual and usages of Hindu religion came
into being, to spread in altered forms east and west

and south. The necessity for this second hypothesis is
twofold. It accounts for the marked ethnical barrier
which separates western from eastern Hindustan.
Elsewhere the various types melt imperceptibly into
one another. Here alone is a definite racial border
line. Again, the theory accounts for the fact that
the Vedic hymns contain no description whatever of
the earlier Aryan migration, and for the fact that the
inhabitants of the middle land always felt a dislike
for the early immigrants as men of low culture and
barbarous manners. For the present, at all events,
and perhaps for all time, Dr Hoernle's ingenious
theory holds the field.

No special theory is required to account for the
physical and mental qualities of the Mongolo-Dra-
vidians of Bengal. No doubt the original population
was Dravidian with a strong intermixture of Tibeto-
Burmese blood, especially in the east and north-east.
But the Hindu religion, developed in the sacred
Midlands round Benares, spread to Bengal, bringing
with it the Indo-European speech which in medieval
times became the copious and supple Bengali tongue.
From the west too came what we in Europe would
call the gentry, the priestly and professional castes.
These have acquired most of the local physical
characters, dusky skin, low stature, round heads.
But in nearly all cases, the fineness and sharp outline
of the nose shows their aristocratic origin, and in

some instances a Bengali Brāhman has all the physical
distinction of a western priest or sage.

When we turn to the Scytho-Dravidian group we
have again to fall back on records of ancient invasions
from the north. Ancient some of them were, but far
less ancient than the settlement of the Aryans in the
north-west. The Sakas have provided India with
one of its many chronological eras ; they founded
dynasties which have left coins behind them, they
have left vague but widely spread traditions. They
were what we Europeans call Scythians. They were
known to the Persians, the Parthians, and the Chinese.
Their original home seems to have been in the south
of China, a land of pre-eminently round-headed races.
We know that they established their dominion over
portions of the Panjāb, Sind, Gujarāt, Rājputānā and
Central India. If they have left traces of their
settlement on their descendants we may reasonably
expect to find round-headed races and tribes in
regions mostly surrounded by long-headed peoples.
Such a zone of broad-headed people does in fact
extend from the western Panjāb right through the
Deccan, till it finally ends in Coorg. Sir H. H.
Risley's theory is that the Scythians first occupied
the great grazing country of the western Panjāb, and
finding their progress eastwards blocked by the Indo-
Aryans, turned southwards, mingled with the Dravidians, and became the ancestors of the warlike

Marātha race. Such an origin forms a tempting
explanation of the well-known predatory habits of
the Marātha hordes, and of their frequent raids all
over the peninsula under the decaying administration
of the later Mogul Emperors. It is an interesting
and fascinating speculation, since it accounts not
only for the physical aspect of the Marāthas but
for their characteristic political genius, for their
wide-ranging forays, their guerilla warfare, their un-
scrupulous dealings, their inveterate love of intrigue,
their clannish habits.

I must here boldly borrow Sir H. H. Risley's
summary of the historical record of Scythian invasions into India, since that is the main justification
for his theory. "In the time of the Achaemenian
kings of Persia," he says, "the Scythians, who were
known to the Chinese as Sse, occupied the regions
lying between the lower course of the Sillis or
Jaxartes and Lake Balkash. The fragments of early
Scythian history which may be collected from classical
writers are supplemented by the Chinese annals,
which tell us how the Sse, originally located in
southern China, occupied Sogdiana and Trans-oxiana
at the time of the establishment of the Graeco-
Bactrian monarchy. Dislodged from these regions
by the Yueh-chi, who had themselves been put to
flight by the Huns, the Sse invaded Bactriana, an
enterprise in which they were frequently allied with

the Parthians. To this circumstance, Ujfalvy says may be due the resemblance which exists between the Scythian coins of India and those of the Parthian kings. At a later period, the Yueh-chi made a further advance, and drove the Sse or Sakas out of Bactriana, whereupon the latter crossed the Paropamisus and took possession of the country called after them Sakastān, comprising Segistān, Arachosia, and Drangiana. But they were left in possession only for a hundred years, for about 25 B.C. the Yueh-chi disturbed them afresh. A body of Scythians then emigrated eastwards, and founded a kingdom in the western portion of the Panjāb. The route they followed in their advance upon India is uncertain ; but to a people of their habits it would seem that a march through Baluchistan would have presented no serious difficulties.

"The Yueh-chi, afterwards known as the Tokhari, were a power in Central Asia and the north-west of India for more than five centuries, from 130 B.C. The Hindus called them Sakas and Turushkas, but their kings seem to have known no other dynastic title than that of Kushan. The Chinese annals tell us how Kitolo, chief of the Little Kushans, whose name is identified with the Kidara of the coins, giving way before the incursion of the Ephthalites, crossed the Paropamisus, and founded, in the year 425 of our era, the kingdom of Gandhāra, of which, in the time

of his son, Peshawar became the capital. About
the same time, the Ephthalites or Ye-tha-ï-li-to of
the Chinese annals, driven out of their territory by the
Yuan-yuan, started westward, and overran in succession Sogdiana, Khwarizan (Khiva), Bactriana, and
finally the north-west portion of India. Their move-
ments reached India in the reign of Skanda Gupta
(452—80) and brought about the disruption of the
Gupta empire. The Ephthalites were known in India
as Huns. The leader of the invasion of India, who
succeeded in snatching Gandhāra from the Kushans
and established his capital at Sākala, is called by the
Chinese Laelih, and inscriptions enable us to identify
him with the original Lakhan Udayāditya of the
coins. His son Toramāna (490—515) took possession
of Gujarāt, Rājputānā, and part of the Ganges valley,
and in this way the Huns acquired a portion of
the ancient Gupta kingdom. Toramāna's successor,
Mihirakula (515—44), eventually succumbed to the
combined attack of the Hindu princes of Mālwā and
Magadha."

I now come to the ethnography as distinguished
from the ethnology of India. Of anthropometry and
the lessons to be learnt from it, I have no personal
experience, and have had to borrow my materials at
second-hand. But with the great system of caste, its
workings, its manifold ramifications, everyone who
has lived in India has come into more or less close

contact. How important caste is in the social life
of the country may be easily inferred from this little
fact. I once asked the late Navin Chandra Sen, then
the most popular of Bengali poets, if he would attempt
a definition of what a Hindu is. After many suggestions, all of which had to be abandoned on closer
examination, the poet came to the conclusion that a
Hindu is (1) one who is born in India of Indian
parents on both sides, and (2) accepts and obeys the
rules of caste. Hinduism is, roughly speaking, the
religion of the Aryo-Dravidians, the upper and fairer
classes among whom regarded the aborigines, matri-
monially, much as white Americans regard their negro
fellow citizens. It has spread over nearly the whole
of India and is still spreading, usually but not always,
carrying with it one of the Indo-European languages
of India. It is the religion and social system of races
and classes which consider themselves intrinsically
superior, and practise a traditional kind of eugenics,
of race preservation. Humbler or more barbarous
races are admitted on various conditions into caste,
sometimes into higher, sometimes into lower positions.
The process is one of that kind of "legal fiction"
with which students of Roman law are familiar. It
is a process of unification and, at the same time, of
social segregation. I have already alluded to the
suggestion that caste-divisions are horizontal, as it
were, compared with the geographical divisions of

races. But it is always dangerous to make general statements about three hundred millions of people scattered over so large an area as India. There are Brāhmans in every part of India, and these usually trace their origin back to the sacred midland where Hinduism came into being. They may be, and probably are, the descendants of the missionaries by whom the religion of the Hindus is, imperceptibly and without open proselytism, spread abroad. Something corresponding to a warrior caste and a caste of scribes is to be found in most provinces, and many of these either claim to be migrants, or have been admitted by adoption into the privileges of warrior or writer blood.

But there are many castes which are purely local, even in name, and are not found elsewhere than in the places where they were admitted into the Hindu community. Many closely printed pages in the Census Reports of each province and state enumerate and describe the thousands of castes revealed by the numbering of the people. It is, of course, only possible to give a very vague and general idea of some of the classes into which the castes of India may conveniently be divided.

I am tempted here to borrow Sir Herbert Risley's definition of caste. But it is a highly abstract definition, and one that cannot be easily carried in the head, even by those who have a practical and familiar acquaintance with members of Indian castes. Roughly a caste is a group of human beings who may not intermarry, or (usually) eat, with members of any other caste. There are also sub-castes which are also endogamous. Very frequently, especially in the parts of India where caste is already an institution of immemorial antiquity, a caste has allotted to it a profession or occupation.

Before we discuss castes properly so called, it is convenient to speak of the tribes of India, since tribes have a tendency to become castes when they come under the pervasive influence of Hindu social ideas. In the south of India are Dravidian tribes, of which the best example are the tribes of Chota Nagpore. These are divided into a number of exogamous groups or clans, calling themselves by the name of an animal or plant, which may be regarded as their totem. The Khonds of Orissa, who once bore an evil name for their practice of human sacrifices to propitiate the earth-goddess, are divided into fifty *gochis* or exogamous clans, each of which bears the name of a village, and believes itself to be descended from a common ancestor. These *gochis* are the nearest known approach to the local exogamous tribe which Mr McLennan and the French sociologists believe to be the earliest form of human society.

The Mongoloid tribes of Assam are much of the same kind, but in many cases, as among the head-hunting Nagas, live at perpetual warfare with one another. In such cases they usually capture their wives in war. It is interesting to note that when population grows too dense for the profitable pursuit of the chase, their principal means of livelihood, such a tribe breaks up into two or more "villages," which immediately begin waging war with one another, which is quite what a French sociologist would expect them to do. I can tell of a case within my own experience in which the headman of a parent village invited the chief of a colony village (his own nephew) to a feast and palaver with his young warriors. The guests were all treacherously put to the sword, as a means of acquiring heads and concubines. I could not get the headman to see that he had been guilty of an atrocious crime. For him, it was lawful strategy. And indeed Naga warfare is merely a series of artfully planned ambushes in which not a few of our own officers perished before we undertook the direct administration of the Naga Hills. Sir H. Risley remarks of this group of tribes that "no very clear traces of totemism have been discovered among them." Subsequent enquiries, however, show that totemistic clans do exist in some of the Assam tribes.

Of the Turko-Iranian tribes of the north-western frontier I need not speak at any length, since these tribes are all sturdy followers of the Prophet, and save that they are under British rule can hardly be

Plate III

Dharkārs
(*Mirzapur district*)

said to belong to India at all. There is no likelihood that they will ever be received into the tolerant bosom of Hinduism, since, to the Indian proper, the Baloch and the Afghan are disagreeable and swaggering caterans, who have an innate scorn for the typical Hindu hierarchy of caste. Among these tribes it is martial ability and valour that win a man consideration and wives.

Let us now turn to caste properly so called, the traditional social divisions of the Hindus. And first it is necessary to say something of the ancient Hindu theory of what caste is, and how it came into existence.

As with the Hebrews, the religious literature of India contains a vast mass of what can only be called law, and perhaps the most famous of Indian law books is the Institutes of Manu, a compilation of rules relating to magic, religion, law, custom, ritual and metaphysics. Even to this day, these branches of speculation and enquiry, so distinct to western imaginations, are apt to be confused together as a result of the pantheistic feeling which pervades Hinduism. The Institutes is a comparatively modern book, but it repeats ideas which are found in a more or less explicit form in early authorities[1]. In this book we are told that in the beginning of things the Pan-theos who "contains all created things and is inconceivable"

[1] The actual date is very uncertain. Dr Burnell thinks the book was composed so late as A.D. 500, but it was probably much older.

produced by effort of thought a golden egg, from
which he himself was born as Brahmā, the creator of
the known universe. From his mouth, his arms,
his thighs, and his feet respectively he created the
four great leading castes, the Brāhman, the Kshatriya,
the Vaiçya, and the Sūdra. These were, briefly, the
priests, the warriors and gentlefolk, the traders, and
the servile classes of human society. The other castes
were gradually formed, the theory states, by intermarriages between these. The three higher castes were
allowed to take wives from lower castes. When the
caste of the mother was next below that of the father,
the child took the caste of his mother and no new caste
was formed. But where the difference of condition
was greater than this, new castes were formed, lower
than those of either parent. Some discrepancies of
rank produced unions which were regarded as peculiarly offensive to human feelings and as tantamount
to incestuous intercourse. These resulted in very
degraded castes. Where the father married beneath
him, the marriage was described as *anuloma* or "with
the hair." When a woman was guilty of a *mésalli-
ance*, the marriage was called *pratiloma* or " against
the hair." The most disgraceful union of this kind
was that between a Brāhman woman and a Sūdra
man, the resulting offspring being relegated to the
caste of Chandāl. The unfortunate Chandāl is described as "that lowest of mortals," and is condemned,

as Sir H. Risley says, to live outside the village, to clothe himself in the garments of the dead, to eat from broken dishes, to execute criminals, and to carry out the corpses of friendless men.

The most superficial acquaintance with existing caste divisions shows that this theory is not so much a hypothesis as a fanciful fiction.   In eastern Bengal, for instance, the Chandāl is evidently a Mongoloid aboriginal, with a considerable strain of Dravidian and perhaps even of Aryan blood.   Yet the fiction shows plainly enough the estimation in which one of the numerically largest divisions of local society is held.   Some thirty years ago, when I was a young magistrate, a comely Chandāl girl appeared before me, her face streaming with blood from a scalp wound.   She asserted gravely that a Sūdra of higher caste had struck her on the head with a stick, because he had found her reading a book as she sat in the doorway of her father's cottage.   I was disinclined to believe this story, but her assailant was promptly sent for, and being brought straight to me, admitted the truth of the charge, and seemed surprised at my indignation at a cowardly assault.

As an attempt to account for the origin and explain the nature of caste the theory of Manu is obviously a failure.   But it contains a picture of the early castes.   It is also interesting because the idea of four original *varnas* or " colours " of men may have been borrowed from the old Persian social organisation. The early scriptures, the Vedas, show that this conception of four original castes was not brought to India by Aryan immigrants. But when caste came into being as a result of the contact of Aryan settlers with Dravidian aborigines, this mythological explanation, which gave such conspicuous eminence to priests and warriors, an eminence already conceded to them on account of the importance of their functions, was readily accepted as a convincing explanation of the hereditary differences between men in society, a difference not merely of function, but of colour, aspect, gesture, speech, breeding, and intelligence. It is necessary to mention this theory, however briefly, since it still holds ground, except among those Indians who have had a European education and even among them has the interest of early and sacred associations which, in Europe, belongs to the cosmological speculations of the book of Genesis.

What, next, are castes as they appear to the eye of the European ethnologist, free from preconceived prejudice, and only anxious to come as near the truth as is possible in his dealings with ancient institutions round which has gathered a vast mass of venerable superstition and religious speculation ? In the first place, castes are often still recognisably *tribes*. Sometimes the leading men of an aboriginal tribe will acquire sufficient wealth and social consideration to wish to obtain the stamp of recognition as reputable Hindus. They will call themselves, for example, and induce their neighbours and the priests of these to call them, Rājputs. They may not at first succeed in intermarrying with true hereditary Rājputs, but in time they will be just Rājputs like any other Rājputs. Or, again, a number of non-Hindus, animists, will join one of the many Hindu sects or fraternities and will intermarry with Vaishnavas, Lingayats, Rāmayats, or other devotees of some favourite deity. Or again, a whole tribe or a considerable portion of a tribe, usually one of some political importance, will enter Hinduism by means of some plausible fiction. The instance quoted by Sir H. Risley is that of the Koches of north-eastern Bengal. These people are Tibeto-Burmans and until recent times spoke a dialect of the agglutinative Bodo language. They now call themselves Rājbansis, "of royal birth," or Bhāngā Kshatriyas, "broken warriors," names which enable them to claim an origin from the traditional dispersion of the Aryan warrior caste by the hero Parasu Rāma, "Rāma of the battle axe." They claim descent from the epic monarch Dasarath, father of Rāma, have their own Brāhmins, and have begun to adopt the Brāhminical system of exogamous *gotras*. But, as Sir H. Risley remarks, they are in a transitional state, since they have all hit upon the same *gotra*, and are therefore compelled to marry within it, except in the rare instances in which they contract unions with Bengali women.

A still more interesting, because more recent, instance of this sort is that of the Meithei, now known to Hindus as Manipuris. In the Mahābhārata is told the tale of how the hero Arjuna wandered from his brethren into Southern and Eastern India, and, among other adventures, met (as Æneas with Dido) with Chitrangadā, the fair daughter of the King of Manipur, somewhere near the eastern coast. Some 150 years ago, the then king of the beautiful valley of Imphāl, between Assam and Burma, was thinking of becoming a Muhammadan, by way of courting the favour of the Muhammadan rulers of Bengal. But Hindu priests persuaded him that a better way of linking his fortunes with those of India, rather than with Ava (with whose royal family his dynasty had usually intermarried), was by becoming Hindu with all his people. Imphāl was identified with Manipur, and many of the Meithei race became Vishnuvite Hindus with their ruler, though they retain their primitive Tibeto-Burman language. I may mention a little personal reminiscence to show how completely the change by fictitious adoption was accepted in Bengal. In 1891, my old friend and chief, Mr Quinton, with all his staff, was treacherously murdered at Manipur. Subsequently when I was magistrate of Chittagong, I found that my head clerk, an extremely mild and intelligent Bengali Kāyastha, had celebrated the easily suppressed mutiny at Manipur by writing a drama based on the ancient legend of Arjuna's amours with Chitrangadā !

Sometimes an aboriginal tribe will become a Hindu caste without losing its old tribal designation. They will worship Hindu gods without daring wholly to neglect tribal deities, which, as might perhaps be expected, are left chiefly to the women of the tribe. Such a tribe will rapidly assimilate itself to the beliefs and practices of Hindu neighbours, and finally only its name and (except in case of occasional intermarriage with other castes) its physical aspect will remain to testify to its origin.

Castes are at present classified as follows :

(1) What Sir H. Risley calls *the tribal type*, instances of which have been given above. Such tribal castes abound in all parts of India. It is not improbable that the great Sūdra division of Hindu tradition was originally the whole mass of Dravidian aboriginals as they came into contact with Aryan immigrants, and were conceded a subordinate place in their social system. It would be useless to give a list of the names of such castes, but I cannot refrain from mentioning the excellent Doms of the Assam Valley, whose name unfortunately associates them with very different people in India proper.

They are obviously of Tibeto-Burman origin, and
deserve closer study than they receive.   Their long
thatched places of worship, true synagogues for
meeting together and curiously unlike the tiny *cellæ*
of Hindu temples, are among the most conspicuous
features of Assam villages.   They have no idols, and
place a *puthi*, a holy book, on what may pass for the
village altar.   They are vaguely Hinduised, but will
humbly declare "*āmi hindu na hô*," "we are not
Hindu folk."   Yet they are well on their way towards
acceptance into caste, and have already a strong
infusion of Hindu blood.

Other border races, though they are still too
savage and independent to become Hindu, are
marked down for absorption.   Such, for instance,
are the Daflas of the northern border of Assam,
cousins of the Abors to whom attention has been
drawn by recent events.   The Daflas are still frankly
animistic ;   their love of strong spirits and other
intoxicants, their addiction to their favourite diet
of roast pork, their extremely uncleanly habits and
barbarous speech, all make them very offensive to
the gentle vegetarian Hindus their neighbours.   But
it happens that the tribal costume closely resembles
the traditional dress of Mahādēva, the Destroyer, the
most active and formidable member of the Hindu
Trinity, and already some Hindus speak of these
genial Highlanders as Siva-bansa, as "of Siva's race."

Many other examples, with interesting details of
fictional methods, will be found in Mr E. A. Gait's
admirable *History of Assam.*

(2) *The functional or occupational type* of caste.
This is the form of caste best known to Europeans,
because, since the first European missionaries and
traders visited those parts of India where the caste
system has had the longest opportunity to evolve,
they came most into contact with this, which is
probably the oldest and most elaborated form of
caste. The Hindu theory of caste encouraged the
adoption of special occupations, and now the evolution has proceeded so far that change of occupation
may usually result in a change of caste. A remarkable instance of this is found in the Marāthi districts
of the Central Provinces. Here is a separate and
newly formed caste of village servants called Gārpa-
gāri, "hail-averters," whose business it is to protect
the village crops from hailstorms. Shepherds who
take to tillage break away from their pastoral
brethren, and so on. Even those who retain their
traditional occupations are wont to adopt more
seemly-sounding names than those that belong to
their trade. I have known barbers who called
themselves Chandra-vaidyas[1], which is a promotion

---

[1] "Moon-physicians," an allusion to the crescent-shaped brass
basin of the barber, such as the helmet of Don Quixote, familiar
to us all.

more subtle than a mere ascent to the status of "hair-dresser," and washermen who have followed suit by dubbing themselves Sukla-vaidya, a word of which "white-worker" is a crude but sufficiently suggestive translation.

(3) The *sectarian type* is a singularly interesting example of the strong social influence of Hindu sentiment. Nearly all new Hindu sects begin by renouncing caste in the enthusiastic following of some single deity, some new explanation of the mysteries of life, and love, and death. These sects are usually the followers of some reforming theorist, whose leadership is apt to become hereditary. Such sects almost always believe that all men are equal, or at all events, that all who accept their doctrines are equal. One of my most interesting recollections is of a now distant interview with a buxom middle-aged lady, the hereditary leader of the Kartā-bhajās of Central Bengal. She sat unveiled, and was accessible to all who, like myself, were interested in the community over which she exercised a firm but good-natured control. It is a picturesque detail that her chosen seat when receiving visitors was an ancient European four-poster bedstead. Her followers (and revenues) were growing rapidly, increased chiefly by the democratic instinct which, even in India, revolts against social prestige. But it would seem that when such a sect grows and

spreads, the old separatist ideas reassert themselves, and the sect breaks up into smaller endogamous communities, whose status depends on the original position of the members in Hinduism. The most remarkable instance of this kind is furnished by the great Lingayat caste of Bombay, which contains over two and a half millions of members. In the twelfth century the Lingayats were a sect who believed in the equality of all men. In Mr P. J. Mead's Bombay Census Report for 1911 is a very interesting account of the present condition of the Lingayats, an account which shows how the scholar, the linguist, and the administrator can work together to find materials for the anthropologist. Dr Fleet's examination of ancient inscriptions has thrown much light on the origin of the sect, but the author of the Report holds that there may be some reason to think that the sect is much older than is commonly supposed.. In any case, they are already divided into three great groups, comprising many subdivisions.

(4) *Castes formed by crossing* come aptly to show that there was some basis for Manu's theory of caste after all. Castes, nowadays, increase by fission, by throwing off sub-castes, and one species of these sub-castes is created by mixed marriages. This tendency, curiously enough, is most evident in Dravidian tribes, such as the Mundās, which are not yet wholly Hinduised, but have been

affected by Hindu example. So far as I know, these mixed castes do not occur among the Mongoloid peoples, and I have come across cases where a member of an aboriginal tribe has been accepted into the caste of a Hindu girl he has married. In one case, within my own experience, the bridegroom had begun as an animist, had become Christian, and finally entered by marriage into the quite respectable Koch caste. One interesting caste in Bengal, that of the Shāgirdpeshas, owes its origin to concubinage with the so-called slaves, the women of tenants surrounding a homestead who pay their rent in service. This, it will be observed, is a caste of illegitimacy, in which the relationship between the legitimate and illegitimate children of a man of good caste is recognised, but the two are not allowed to eat together. The classical instance of a mixed caste is the Khas of Nepāl, said to be the result of very ancient intermarriages between Rājput or Brāhman immigrants and the Mongolian "daughters of men."

(5) *Castes of the national type.* This somewhat daring title we owe to the great authority of Sir H. Risley. As one instance, he mentions the Newārs, a Mongoloid people, who were once the ruling race in Nepāl, till the Gurkha invasion in 1769, and have now become a caste. Other instances might be found on the north-eastern frontier. But the people

Plate IV

Banjara women
(*Mirzapur district*)

Sir Herbert Risley had in mind when he invented
this term was undoubtedly the remarkable Marātha
race, once the most daring warriors and freebooters
in India, and now the rivals of the Bengalis in intellectual ability, and probably more than their
equals in political sagacity. Sir Rāmkrishna Gopāl
Bhandārkar is our authority for the statement that
the Rattas were a tribe who held political supremacy
in the Deccan from the earliest days. In time they
became Mahā-rattas, "Great Rattas," and the land
in which they lived was called Mahārattha, which,
by a common linguistic habit of mankind, was
Sanskritised into Mahā-rāshtra. Their marriage
customs show marked traces of totemistic institutions. An extremely interesting account of the
present condition of this warlike and enterprising
race will be found at pp. 289, 290 of the Bombay
Census Report for 1911. It neither supports nor
discourages Sir H. Risley's ingenious theory of the
Scythic origin of the Marāthas, which is at least
a theory which recognises the respect in which our
ancestors held their martial prowess and talents[1].

(6) *Castes formed by migration.* These are new
castes which serve to enforce the warning against
a too ready acceptance of the definition of caste as
a "horizontal" division of humanity. It is a method
of forming new communities of Hindus which is very

---

[1] But see the postscript to this chapter.

easily intelligible to us, seeing that our own race is split into sections only differing from castes in not being strictly endogamous, such as Anglo-Indians, Australians, New Zealanders, and so forth. Members leave home and settle among strangers. They are assumed to have formed foreign habits, eaten strange food, worshipped alien gods, and have a difficulty— an expensive difficulty—in finding wives in the parent caste. After a time they marry only among themselves, become a sub-caste, and are often known by some territorial name, Bārendra, Rārhi, or what not. Such seemingly are the remarkable Nāmbudri Brāhmans of Malabar, and the Rārhi Brāhmans of Bengal. Sometimes change of habitat brings about loss of rank, sometimes promotion. These are matters on which the Census Reports now being published are full of interesting details. But they are matters which are not easily summarised. No doubt Mr Gait's Report on the combined results of Census operations in India will show the progress of castes of this type during the last ten years.

(7) *Castes formed by changes of custom.* This is a fruitful cause of new divisions of Hindu society. It is, for the moment, more than usually operative, owing to the spread of education, and often represents a difference of social opinion which corresponds, more or less closely, to Conservative and Radical ideas among ourselves. It evidently was always a

cause of fissiparous tendencies. The most notable instance is the distinction between Jāts and Rājputs, both apparently sprung from the same stock, but separated socially, amongst other causes, by the fact that the former practise and the latter abjure infant marriages.

This is a very rapid and highly summarised account of the races and castes of India. There are many obvious omissions. Nothing has been said of the Sikhs, little or nothing about the numerous races of the north-eastern frontier. But enough has been said to give a fair general impression of what the physical characters of the Indian peoples are, and what kind of institution caste is in its practical working. More might have been said about totemistic clans, but on this subject those who would pursue their studies further have only to turn to Dr J. G. Frazer's work on the subject. In the next chapter, I have to borrow my materials from Sir G. A. Grierson, and show how the peoples of India are divided by differences of language. On the whole, those linguistic divisions correspond with remarkable accuracy to the orographical and climatic structure of the country and the racial divisions which we owe to the learning and ingenuity of Sir H. H. Risley. Where there are great open plains, watered and fertilised by mighty rivers, we get large populations speaking the great literary languages of India. In the rugged recesses of the mountains we find small communities, divided from one another by physical obstacles which have produced rigid local patriotisms and enmities, and a wonderful variety of savage speeches. The linguist has usually worked independently of the ethnologist, and has come to his own unprejudiced conclusions. It is interesting to find how closely the results of their separate enquiries agree.

Postscript.

Sir H. H. Risley's theory as to the Scythian origin of the Marāthas has not passed unquestioned, and those who wish to see a brief and clear account of the latest theories on the subject should read Mr Crooke's paper on "Rājputs and Marāthas" in Vol. XL. (January—June, 1910) of the *Journal of the Royal Anthropological Institute.* Mr Crooke, who gives copious references to the latest literature on the subject, holds that "the theory that a Hun or Scythian element is to be traced in the population of the Deccan is inconsistent with the facts of tribal history, so far as they can now be ascertained." Mr Crooke thinks that the anthropometrical facts can be explained otherwise than by Saka invasion and an infusion of Scythian blood. "The presence of a brachycephalic strain," he says, "in Southern and

Western India need not necessarily imply a Mongoloid invasion from Central Asia. The western coast
was always open to the entry of foreign races. Intercourse with the Persian Gulf existed from a very
early period, and Mongoloid Akkads or the short-
headed races from Baluchistan may have made their
way along the coast or by sea into Southern and
Western India. But it is more probable that this
strain reached India in prehistoric times, and that
the present population is the result of the secular
intermingling of various race types, rather than of
events within the historical period." Mr Crooke's
view is supported by the recently issued Census
Report of the Bombay Presidency, which says, "the
term Marātha is derived by some from two Sanskrit
words, *mahā*, ' great,' and *rathi*, ' a warrior.' "
According to Sir Rāmkrishna Gopāl Bhandārkar it
is derived from Rattas, a tribe which held political
supremacy in the Deccan from the remotest time.
"The Rattas called themselves Mahā Rattas or Great
Rattas, and thus the country in which they lived
came to be called Mahārāttha, the Sanskrit of which
is Mahā-rāshtra."

Indigenous names are frequently Sanskritised,
much as we turn French *chaussée* into "causeway."
Sometimes the change is so complete that the
original cannot be identified. In some cases the
alteration is easily recognised. In Northern Bengal,

for instance, is the river *Ti-stā*, a name which belongs
to a large group of Tibeto-Burman river names beginning with *Ti-*, or *Di-*, such as *Ti-pai, Di-bru,
Di-kho, Di-sāng*, etc., etc.   Hindus say the name
Ti-stā is either a corruption of Sanskrit *Tri-srotas*,
"having three streams," or of Tṛṣṇā, "thirst." Etymo-
logy and legend, in fact, give but doubtful guidance
to the ethnologist, and the best hope of acquiring
some real knowledge of Rājput and Marātha origins
lies in the possible discovery of coins and inscriptions in the absence of direct historical records.

CHAPTER II

THE LANGUAGES OF INDIA

It is quite possible to live many years in one
province or another of India without obtaining more
than the vaguest conception of the linguistic riches
of the country.   It was Sir G. A. Grierson who
rendered it impossible for any but the most careless
to ignore the fact that India has not only more
languages than Europe, but many more kinds and
families of speech.   Most Europeans in India live in
the populous areas where ethnical and geographical
conditions are favourable to the evolution and spread
of one of the great literary languages.   In Madras,
the European comes into contact with one or other

of the cultivated Dravidian tongues. In Bombay, he learns that Marāthi and Gujarāti have ancient and interesting literatures. In Calcutta, he is surrounded by millions of Bengalis, who in modern times have as many varieties of literary expression as the most advanced of European races. In Rangoon, he hears the most highly organised of Tibeto-Burman speeches. In Allahabad, Benares, Lahore, Patna, he acquires some smattering of the beautiful and expressive languages which are closest to the model of the original Indo-Aryan idiom. These are the exact counter parts of the great literary languages of Europe, of English, French, German, Italian, etc. But while the European mountains contain one or two shy survivals at most of primitive ways of talking, India has many languages of the type of Basque. In the little frontier province of Assam alone, dozens of grammars and vocabularies have been printed, and much more remains to be done. Happily, an appetite for more information has been aroused by the feast spread before linguists in Sir G. A. Grierson's great *Survey*. He himself is at work on a book which will tell us all that is at present known about the many languages of India, and their relations with one another. But in addition to his own labours, Sir George Grierson has been an apostle of linguistic research and has gathered round him many disciples, not all of whom recognise whence came the impulse

that has set them to an examination of the history
and growth of Indian languages.   Most promising
sign of all, native scholars no longer disdain the
living tongues of India, nor confine their studies to
the classics of Sanskrit, Arabic, and Persian.   In
Bengal alone, the Proceedings of the *Vangiya Sāhitya
Parisat*, a society for the pursuit of linguistic and
ethnological research, now form a goodly library of
books, and the poet, Rabindranath Tagore, whose
own English version of his charming *Gitanjali* is in
the hands of all who love poetry or are interested
in Indian matters, is also a very keen and competent
student of his native language on lines suggested by
the enquiries of European scholars.   Much has been
learnt, but linguistic research in India has still many
interesting secrets for the zeal of European students to
reveal.   In Scandinavia, Germany, France, a new sense
of the value of such studies has been aroused.   All
that can be attempted in the following pages is to show,
very summarily and briefly, what is known at present.

We have already seen that there are seven more
or less recognisable types of Indian humanity.   To
these roughly correspond five great families of living
vernaculars. The Turko-Iranian, the Indo-Aryan, the
Scytho-Dravidian, the Aryo-Dravidian, and the Mongolo-Dravidian races have for the most part acquired
Aryan languages which, in their relations to Sanskrit
and Persian, may be compared with the Romance

languages of Europe in their relations to literary Greek and Latin. The Dravidian races speak one or other of the great Dravidian dialects, or some idiom of the Mundā languages of Chota Nagpore. Among the Mongoloid races of the extreme north and east of India, we find the Mon-Khmer and the Tibeto-Chinese families of speech. Of these, the Dravidian family seems to be confined to India—to the high tablelands of Southern India, with one outlying settlement among the Brāhuis of Baluchistan. This Dravidian speech would seem to be the original and indigenous language of India. The Mundā languages of Chota Nagpore, again, are plainly very ancient Indian tongues and are, in all probability, as aboriginal as the true Dravidian speech. But Mundā tongues have elements in common with the Mon-Khmer languages of Further India, Malacca, and Australonesia. The present explanation of this fact is provided by the supposition that, in prehistoric times, these distant regions shared a common language with great part of Northern India. But, for all practical purposes, the relations of the Mundā languages with the Far East are still so vaguely defined, that they may be provisionally regarded as being as indigenous as their neighbours, the Dravidian languages. The connection of the Mon-Khmer languages with Further India and the Pacific have formed the subject of the now famous researches of Pater

Schmidt of Vienna and other German investigators. The Indo-Chinese family of languages is obviously connected with the many dialects of Southern China. An Indian journalist once told me that he thought that the tumbled mountain ranges which separate India from China and form, for the time, a semi-savage "no man's land" of primitive social customs and administration, are the most interesting area on earth. It is an Asiatic and a huger Albania, of whose ethnological and linguistic condition much has yet to be learned. Those who heard Mr Archibald Rose's lectures in London and Cambridge on his travels in these regions will easily realise how much room there is here for anthropological and linguistic research among the rough but attractive races of this quarter.

Lastly, in the great alluvial plain which separates the Himalayas from the tableland of the south, and along the western coast, are the peoples who use one or other of the great Aryan vernaculars, languages of much the same type as the modern languages of Europe, sharing much of their vocabulary, and ultimately derived from similar if still obscure origins. It is of all these languages, and of some of their innumerable dialects (not all of them even now known by name), that some account must be given in this chapter.

The history of the languages of India has reflected the long struggle for pre-eminence between the

indigenous Dravidian culture of the south and the
Aryan civilisation of the north. The Mundā languages
are those of an isolated group of highlanders, who, till
quite recent times, hardly came into contact with or
were influenced by the speech or thought of other
races. The Mon-Khmer-speaking people of the Khasi
Hills were similarly wholly isolated, and were long
supposed to be absolutely aboriginal and separate
from other races of men, till quite recent investigations discovered their linguistic affinities with the
Mons of Southern Burma and races in French Indo-
China. The Tibeto-Burman languages of the north-
eastern frontier are the simple and primitive speech
of semi-savage men.   For such languages, contact
with the Aryan languages means rapid decay and
dissolution.

Hindu civilisation and Hindu religion find easy
converts in the rude and simple Mongoloid people
of the north-east, and acceptance of Hindu manners
and customs almost always results in a rapid change
of language.   So again, the Iranian languages represent the final stage in the advance of Islam and
its languages as a conquering religion.   The Iranian
tongues of the north-western frontier are only Indian
in the fact that they happen to fall within the administrative border of British India.   If we omit all
consideration of these races and languages for the
present, we shall be free to consider the long struggle

between the Aryan and the Dravidian. The Aryan
religion, the religion of the Hindus, has spread all
over India, and as the Dravidian temples of the south
are among the glories of Hindu religious architecture,
so the Hinduism of the south is now, in many ways,
the most typical and interesting form of the religion.
The spread of the Aryan blood has been far less wide
in extent, as the previous chapter sufficiently shows.
The Aryan languages have spread all over the north
of India, up to an irregular line running obliquely
across the peninsula from near Vizagapatam on the
east coast to near Goa on the west coast. Into the
Aryan area projects the rocky plateau of Chota
Nagpore, where the Mundā dialects still survive,
and there are a few other outlying areas where
Dravidian tribes still use the original language of
India. With these exceptions, Northern India, from
Bombay to Calcutta now speaks Aryan languages.

Let me then begin by giving a brief account of
the two ancient and indigenous families of language
in India, the Dravidian and Mundā families. Sir
G. Grierson's *Survey* has definitely established the
fact that, in spite of the close physical resemblance
between the Dravidian races properly so called and
the inhabitants of Chota Nagpore, there is no
linguistic affinity between them. In Sir George
Grierson's own words " they differ in their pronunciation, in their modes of indicating gender, in their

Plate V

Seoris or Savaras
(*Mirzapur district*)

declensions of nouns, in their method of indicating the relationship of a verb to its objects, in their numeral systems, in their principles of conjugation, in their methods of indicating the negative, and in their vocabularies. The few points in which they agree are points which are common to many languages scattered all over the world."

(1) The *Dravidian languages.* These are, as aforesaid, the languages of Southern India. Two of them survive further to the north in Chota Nagpore and the Sonthal Parganas, where they exist side by side with Mundā dialects. One curiously isolated Dravidian language is Brāhui, an extraordinary survival, far to the north-west, in the midst of the Iranian and Muhammadan languages of Baluchistan. The Sanskrit writers knew of two great southern languages which they named the Andhra-bhāshā and the Drāvida-bhāshā. The first corresponded to what is now Telugu and its cognates, the latter to the rest of the southern languages. Sir George Grierson classifies the Dravidian family thus :

					Number of speakers (1901)
A.	Drāvida group:				
	Tamil	.	.	.	. 16,525,500
	Malayalam	.	.	.	. 6,029,304
	Kanarese	.	.	.	. 10,365,047
	Kodagu	.	.	.	. 39,191

						Number of speakers (1901)
	Tulu	.	.	.	.	535,210
	Toda	.	.	.	.	805
	Kota	.	.	.	.	1300
	Kurukh	.	.	.	.	592,351
	Malto	.	.	.	.	60,777
B.	Intermediate languages:					
	Gond, etc.	.	.	.	.	1,123,974
C.	Andhra group:					
	Telugu	.	.	.	.	20,696,872
	Kandh	.	.	.	.	494,099
	Kolami	.	.	.	.	1505
D.	Brāhui	.	.	.	.	48,589
						56,514,524

Sir G. Grierson borrows the following general account of the main characteristics of the Dravidian forms of speech, with slight verbal alterations, from the *Manual of the Administration of the Madras Presidency*:

"In the Dravidian languages all nouns denoting inanimate substances and irrational beings are of the neuter gender. The distinction of male and female appears only in the pronoun of the third person, in adjectives formed by suffixing the pronominal terminations, and in the third person of the verb. In all other cases, the distinction of gender is marked by separate words signifying 'male' and 'female.' Dravidian nouns are inflected, not by means of case terminations, but by means of suffixed postpositions and separable particles. Dravidian neuter nouns are rarely pluralized; Dravidian languages use postpositions instead of prepositions. Dravidian adjectives are incapable of declension. It is characteristic of these languages, in contradistinction to Indo-European, that, wherever practicable, they use as adjectives the relative participles of verbs, in preference to nouns of quality or adjectives properly so called. A peculiarity of the Dravidian (and also of the Munḍā) dialects is the existence of two pronouns of the first person plural, one inclusive of the person addressed, the other exclusive. The Dravidian languages have no passive voice, this being expressed by verbs signifying 'to suffer' etc. The Dravidian languages, unlike the Indo-European, prefer the use of continuative participles to conjunctions. The Dravidian verbal system possesses a negative as well as an affirmative voice. It is a marked peculiarity of the Dravidian languages that they make use of relative participial nouns instead of phrases introduced by relative pronouns. These participles are formed from the various participles of the verb by the addition of a formative suffix. Thus 'the person who came' is in Tamil literally 'the who-came'."

It is worth while, for once, to quote this somewhat technical description because it shows that though the Aryan languages have driven the Dravidian languages out of Northern India, the latter may have affected the Aryan speech in the transition which, in common with the corresponding speeches of Europe, it has undergone from inflected to analytic ways of talking.

Tamil. Tamil, or Arava, is spoken all over the south of India and the northern part of Ceylon. It extends as far as Mysore on the west coast and Madras on the east coast. It has been carried all over Further India by emigrant coolies. As might be expected from its geographical position, it is the oldest, richest, and most highly organised of Dravidian languages. It has an extensive literature written in a literary dialect called "Shen" or "perfect" as compared with the colloquial "Kodum" or "rude" speech of ordinary men. The words "Tamil" and "Drāvida" are both corruptions of an original "Drānida." Tamil has an alphabet of its own.

Malayalam. Malayalam is a branch of Tamil which came into existence in the ninth century A.D. It is the language of the Malabar coast, and has one dialect, Yerava, spoken in Coorg. This language has borrowed its vocabulary freely from Sanskrit. It differs from the mother tongue in having dropped the personal terminations of verbs. Its alphabet is the Grantha character, much used in Southern India for writing Sanskrit.

Kanarese. Kanarese is the language of the Kingdom of Mysore and the adjoining British territory. It has an ancient literature written in a character resembling that of Telugu. Its dialects of Badaga and Kurumba are spoken in the Nīlgiri hills. Kodagu, the language of Coorg, is said by some to be a dialect of Kanarese, and is the link between it and Tulu, the language of part of South Kanara in Madras. Toda and Kota will always have an interest for anthropologists in connection with Dr Rivers' now classical investigation into the social life of the Todas.

Gond. The Gond language is spoken outside the true Dravidian area, in the hill country of Central India. It is intermediate between the Drāvida and Andhra languages, and like most hill languages has many dialects. It is unwritten and has no literature.

Telugu. Telugu is the only important Andhra language now surviving. It is the language of the eastern coast from Madras to near the southern border of Orissa. It has an extensive literature written in a character of its own, adapted from the Aryan Devanāgari. This character, like the writing of Orissa, is easily recognised by its loops and curves, said to be due to the difficulty of writing straight lines with a stylus on a palm leaf without splitting the leaf.

Finally there remains the isolated and distant Brāhui language in Baluchistan. Its separate existence has led to a very pretty quarrel between linguists and ethnologists. Dr Haddon in his work on the *Wanderings of Peoples*, in this series, says that "the Dravidians may have been always in India : the significance of the Brahui of Baluchistan, a small tribe speaking a Dravidian language, is not understood, probably it is merely a case of cultural drift." Sir George Grierson says "if they (the Dravidians) came from the north-west, we must look upon the Brāhuis as the rear-guard; but if from the south, they must be considered as the advance guard of the Dravidian immigration. Under any circumstances it is possible that the Brāhuis alone retain the true Dravidian ethnic type, which has been lost in India proper by admixture with other aboriginal nationalities such as the Mundas." My own diffident suggestion is that the Brāhuis may be a Dravidian race as a survival of emigration when Northern India was also Dravidian, as the French are a "Latin" race.

Of the Mundā languages I need not speak at any length, interesting as they are to students of spoken speech. They are spoken by over three millions of people, and, besides numerous dialects of each, are six in number. They have been carefully studied by missionaries and others, and many of them are now recorded in the Roman character.

I must apologise for a somewhat dull and detailed account of the Dravidian languages. It seemed necessary to explain what manner of languages they were that fought an unequal and not always losing fight with the great Aryan languages of the north. The account of the struggle between the two, on the other hand, has an enduring interest. Dravidian and Aryan languages now face one another much as do French and Breton in Brittany, English and Gaelic in the Highlands, Flemish and French in Belgium. But in the Indian plains the contest was waged on a much vaster scale, and some of the incidents of the long struggle can still be recovered. One point should be carefully borne in mind. In Northern India the Aryan languages and the Hindu religion are openly and completely victorious. The peculiar philosophic and religious ideas of Hinduism find apt and copious expression in the Aryan vocabulary of the north. But Dravidian India, too, in accepting Hinduism, perforce accepted with it much of the Aryan vocabulary. It is Dravidian still, as England is still mainly Germanic. But without Aryan words it could hardly give expression to Hindu speculations and aspirations. As our own language, as these words I write, have a strong intermixture of Latin phrase and idiom, so the Aryan influence has in a greater or less degree penetrated to Ceylon itself, once held by Aryan poets to be the home of demoniac

5—2

and barbarian races. There are Dravidian traces
in the north, survivals of old days of Dravidian
supremacy. In the south, a veneer of Aryan culture
has been added to the ancient Dravidian civilisation.
This was strong to resist a change of idiom : it clung
sturdily to most of its vocabulary ; but there has
been an infusion of Aryan words, needed for ritual
and, in some cases, for administrative purposes. The
use of the word "administrative" reminds me to say,
before passing on, that nowhere in India is English
so freely used as in the Dravidian south. Originally
Englishmen seem to have found Dravidian languages
too difficult a means of communication. But Dravidians themselves soon discovered that English was
a convenient *lingua franca.* All India is now making
the same discovery, and English is binding the educated
classes into a new pan-Indian race.

The Aryan Languages.

We now return to the fascinating story of the
spread of the Indo-Aryan languages over the north
and west of the peninsula. In the tale, captured
from the patient study of words and idioms, and
finding only occasional support from legend, and
practically none from history, since history had not
yet begun to exist, we get a singularly moving and
interesting picture of the social existence of vanished

tribes of men. We partly know and partly conjecture that there was once a race of men whom we may conveniently call Indo-Europeans who spoke the parent-speech of the modern languages of Europe, Armenia, Persia, and northern India. Probably the Panjāb in very early times was occupied by several immigrations of Indo-European folk, for in the earliest days of which we have any knowledge, the land of the Five Rivers is already the home of many Indo-Aryan tribes, who live at enmity with one another, and have a fraternal habit of speaking of one another as unintelligible barbarians.

In the Sanskrit geography of somewhat later times, India is divided into the sacred Madhya-deça, the "Midland," and the rest. Already this Midland country, the home of the latest immigrants, is considered to be the true habitat of civilised Aryans, all the rest of the peninsula being more or less barbarous. It is important that the reader should understand exactly where this Midland lay. On the north it ended below the foot-slopes of the Himalayas. On the south, it was bordered by the Vindhyā hills, the southern boundary of the Gangetic plain. On the west it extended to Sirhind on the eastern limits of what is now the Panjāb. On the east its limit was the confluence of the Ganges and Jumna. Its inhabitants, of mixed Aryan and Dravidian origin, had spread eastwards from the upper part of the *do-āb*, the watershed between the two rivers. Their language gradually became the current speech of the Midland. It was cultivated as a literary tongue from early times and came to be known as Sanskrit, the "purified" language. Purified and systematised it was by the labours of grammarians and phoneticians, the most famous of whom is Pānini, who lived and wrote about 300 B.C.

To the phonetic acumen of these early grammarians the existing alphabets of northern India, singularly different in arrangement from the confused order of European and Semitic letters, bear testimony. In the Indian alphabets the letters are arranged in order, according to the vocal organs chiefly used in their pronunciation, as Gutturals, Palatals, Cerebrals, Dentals, and Labials. All the phonetic changes which occur in the formation of the numerous compound words are carefully reduced to rule, and the spelling professes to be (what perhaps no spelling ever has been or can be) phonetic.

It is a moot point whether Sanskrit was in Pānini's time a spoken vernacular. It is more probable that it was, what it still remains in most parts of Hindu India, a second and literary language, used much as Latin was used in medieval Europe. The spoken form of the archaic language found in the older Vedas developed into Prākrit, which existed side by side with Sanskrit as the spoken dialects of Italy

existed side by side with literary Latin. As the
Italian dialects developed into the modern languages
of Europe, so the Prākrits gave birth to the Aryan
modern languages of India. Thus the latter were
not in any accurate sense derived from Sanskrit, but
only shared a common origin with it[1]. It remained,
however, as a standard of literary perfection and
was destined to play an important part in the en-
richment of many of the modern languages of India,
when contact with western culture brought about
what may fairly be called a literary renaissance.
This was particularly the case with Bengali. Its
medieval literature was all but confined to rhymed
hymns and tales. English education led to a revival
of Sanskrit studies. From England Bengal learnt
that it was possible to write prose in many varied
forms, in novels, essays, histories, journalism, and so
forth. The medieval literary language, derived from
the Prākrit, had grown insufficient for the expression
of anything but the simplest devotional or amatory
emotion, and Bengali borrowed freely from the rich
treasury of Sanskrit.

In the "Midland," then, were various forms of
Prākrit, side by side with the sacred and literary
Sanskrit. Round the Midland, on the west, south,

---

[1] As in Europe, the modern Aryan languages differ from one
another chiefly in survivals from the indigenous earlier speech
which preceded each of them.

and east lay territories inhabited by other Indo-Aryan
tribes. This country included what is now the Panjāb,
Sind, Gujarāt, Rājputānā and the country to its east,
Oudh and Bihār. The tribes inhabiting this semi-
circular tract had each of them its own dialect. But
it is important to note that the dialects of this "Outer
Band" were much more closely related to one another
than to the spoken language of the "Midland." It
was this circumstance which suggested Dr Hoernle's
ingenious theory, already mentioned, of the second
and separate invasion of Aryans into the Midland
over the mountainous passes of Gilgit, too high,
arduous, and difficult to be traversed by the families
and herds of the nomad newcomers.

In course of time the population of the Midland
grew in numbers and valour and pressed closely on
the food supplies of the tract. It was already the
centre of a vigorous and widely influential civilisation.
It contained the imperial cities of Delhi and Kanauj,
and the sacred city of Mathura (Μόδουρα ἡ τῶν θεῶν,
as Ptolemy calls it). This crowded, vigorous, and
martial population was bound to expand. It spread
into the eastern Panjāb, Rājputānā, Gujarāt and
Oudh, carrying with it its language. Hence, as Sir
George Grierson points out, we get in this "Outer
Band" mixed languages, of the Midland type near
the "Midland" centre, but fading into local dialects
as we go further west, south, and east. Finally as the

Plate VI

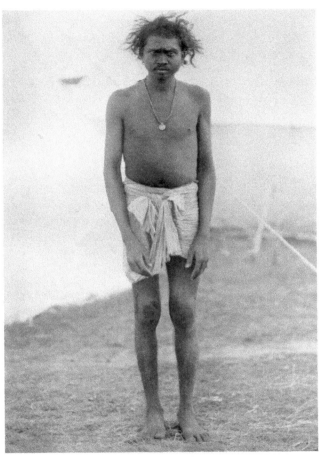

A Bhuiyār
(*Mirzapur district*)

Midlanders crowded into the territories of the Outer
Band, the inhabitants of these took refuge among the
Dravidians of the south and east, and so gave birth
to dialects which ultimately became Marāthi in the
south and Oriyā, Bengali and Assamese on the east, all
of them characteristic languages of the "Outer Band."

I am borrowing so freely and unscrupulously from
Sir George Grierson that it is a relief to pause for a
moment to interpose a very diffident suggestion of
my own. Vocabulary, and even idiom, have become
a dubious guide to the constituent elements of the
"Outer Band" languages which have almost entirely
destroyed the original vocabularies of the Dravidian or
Mongolo-Dravidian races who use them. But it is just
possible that accentuation, rhythm, metre may furnish
some clue to these vanished dialects, which may have
bequeathed a characteristic tone of voice to their
Aryan successors. Bengali, for instance, has a very
peculiar initial phrasal accent which strongly distinguishes it from the etymologically cognate speech
of Bihār, much as the characteristic *accent tonique*
of French distinguishes it from Italian and Spanish.
Native scholars in Bengal are, I am glad to say,
beginning to work at the Dravidian elements in their
expressive and copious language, and will, I hope,
soon investigate the Mongolian elements, whether of
idiom or pronunciation, in the Bengali of the north-
eastern part of the province.

To return to Sir George Grierson, he holds
that the present linguistic condition of northern
India is this:—there is, firstly, a Midland Indo-
Aryan language which holds the Gangetic Doāb.
Round it on three sides is a band of Mixed languages, in the eastern Panjāb, Gujarāt, Rājputānā
and Oudh. With these Sir George includes the
Indo-Aryan languages of the Himalayan slopes
north of the Midland, which have been introduced
in comparatively recent times by immigrants from
Rājputānā.

The Prākrits. Before I leave the Aryan languages
of India, I must give a brief summary of what Sir
George Grierson says of the Prākrits, the spoken
speeches which have always, implicitly 'or ex-
plicitly, been distinguished from the artificial and
literary Sanskrit. The Primary Prākrits of the
Midland and Outer Band (of which latter no record
survives) were of the same type as the Latin known
to us in literature. They were synthetic and inflected
languages. These gradually decayed (or developed)
into what Sir G. Grierson calls the Secondary Prākrits.
These are still synthetic, but diphthongs and harsh
combinations of consonants are avoided, "till in the
latest developments we find a condition of almost
absolute fluidity, each language becoming an emascu-
lated collection of vowels hanging for support on an
occasional consonant." These Secondary Prākrits

lasted from the days of the Buddha (550 B.C.) to about 1000 A.D.

One at least of these Secondary Prākrits, Pāli, has obtained world-wide fame as the language of the Buddhist scriptures. Thus crystallised, it underwent the same fate as Sanskrit and became more or less what we call in Europe a "dead" language. In the Midland was a great and famous Prākrit called Sauraseni, after the Sanskrit name, Surasena, of the country round Mathura. In Bihār was Māgadhī; in Oudh and Baghelkhand was Ardha-māgadhī or "half Māgadhī"; south of these was Mahārāshtri, which is best known to students of the ancient Indian drama as the vehicle of the lyrics with which the plays are studded. Kings, sages, heroes and other noble characters speak Sanskrit. Inferior personages use Sauraseni.

The Secondary Prākrits themselves degenerated into what Indian grammarians call Apabhramsas, "corrupt" or "decayed" tongues, which were used for literary purposes and finally became the parents of the great Aryan languages of the present time.

For comparison with the preceding table of the Dravidian languages, I give below the census table of the Aryan languages as recorded in 1901 :—

Number of
speakers

A. Language of the Midland:
   Western Hindi 40,714,925

Number of
speakers

B. Intermediate languages.

    a. More nearly related to the Midland language:

Rājasthānī	10,917,712
The Pahārī (or 'mountain') languages of the	
Himalaya	3,124,981
Gujarāti	9,439,925
Panjābi	17,070,961

    b. More nearly related to the Outer languages:

Eastern Hindi	22,136,358

C. Outer languages.

    a. North-western group:

Kāshmīrī	1,007,957
Kohistānī	36
Lahndā	3,337,917
Sindhī	3,494,971

    b. Southern language:

Marāthī	18,237,899

    c. Eastern group:

Bihārī	34,579,844
Oriyā	9,687,429
Bengali	44,624,048
Assamese	1,350,846

Of all these modern languages, their idioms, their
characters, their literature, I do not venture to give
even a summarised account. Those who have any
curiosity to learn more about them cannot do better
than consult Sir George Grierson's work on *The
Languages of India*, until it, in its turn, is superseded
by the book he is now writing from the materials

collected in his *Linguistic Survey.* But everyone
who has read *The Newcomes* will want to know what
Hindustāni is, especially as it is one of the languages
prescribed for the study of probationers for the
Indian Civil Service and is taught at the universities
of Oxford, Cambridge, London, and Dublin. In the
strictest sense Hindustāni is the dialect of western
Hindi spoken between Meerut and Delhi. It was
much cultivated, as a literary dialect, by both Hindus
and Musalmāns. The latter wrote, and write it,
in the Persian character, and have added a large
number of Persian and Arabic words. In this
Persianised form it is known as Urdū, "a name
derived from the *Urdū-e mu 'alla,* or royal military
bazaar outside the imperial palace at Delhi, where it
is supposed to have had its origin." Under Muhammadan rule Urdū was almost as much the *lingua franca*
of India as English has come to be in modern times.

Another point is worth noting here. The Aryan
languages of northern India are, in a very real sense,
Hindu languages. Perhaps I shall make myself clearer
by asserting that the languages of Western Europe
are Christian languages. For historical reasons, their
religious phraseology has a Christian connotation and
allusiveness. But in the west, the distinction between
things secular and things religious has become so
familiar that the Christian element in our speech is
not recognisable in our ordinary talk. In Hindu

India, on the other hand, almost every act of a man's life has some religious or superstitious significance, and hence all the Aryan languages in the mouths of Hindus are markedly different from the shape they assume when spoken by Musalmāns.   In the case of western Hindi we have the recognised Muhammadan dialect of Urdū, but in other languages too there is a Muhammadan dialect or *patois*, even if it has no separate name.   A curious exception, however, occurs in eastern Bengal, where the bulk of the population is Musalmān.   In this region the Muhammadans are comparatively recent converts from the lower aboriginal or Mongoloid castes, whose Muhammadanism sits very lightly on their habits and consciences, and so far as my own experience goes, there is little difference between the speech of the lower Musalmāns and their friends and cousins the Chandāls and other indigenous castes.

The Indo-Chinese Languages.

Finally, I must say a few words about the Indo-Chinese and Mon-Khmer languages.   I spent most of my official life among people speaking these languages, and find, somewhat shamefacedly, that Sir G. A. Grierson makes me responsible for sundry vocabularies compiled in my distant youth.   Naturally, I feel a personal interest in the people of the north-

eastern border, and am tempted to enlarge on their
qualities of speech and character.   But I have left
myself little space, and the Mongoloid races of the
frontier are hardly Indian in any proper sense of the
word.   Moreover, though their total number is not
great, they speak many languages.   The Census of
1901 recognises 119 such languages.   The most important of them all is, of course, Burmese, which is
spoken by about seven and a half millions of people.
There are nearly 900,000 Karens in Burma, and
about 750,000 Shans.   The Meithei (now Manipuris)
mentioned above are 272,997 in number.   The Boro
or Kachari people of the Assam valley, a most attractive and delightful race, number somewhat less than
250,000.   The other languages of this type have
mostly a much smaller number of speakers than these.
But mention should be made of 250,000 Mons, Pa-
lungs and Was in Burma, and 177,827 Khāsis in
Assam, since these constitute the only members of
the Mon-Khmer family still found within the limits
of British India.

These people, speaking Indo-Chinese languages,
surround India proper on the north and east in a
crescent-shaped curve, mostly in the valleys of lofty
and rugged mountains.   From the eastern mountains
projects into the midst of the modern province of
Assam a range of hills, dividing the valley of the
Brahmaputra from that of Sylhet, which is watered

by the Surma. Readers of Sir W. W. Hunter's delightful little book on *The Thackerays in India* will not need to be told where Sylhet is, or what sort of a place it is. This range of hills is inhabited by the Garos on the west, and the Nagas on the east, both Tibeto-Burman races. Between them, on one of the most beautiful plateaus in the world, are the Khāsis, once, as I have said elsewhere, regarded as being as isolated and unique as our European Basques, but now proved to be, linguistically at least, connected with the Mons in Burma, and many races and tribes in Further India and Australonesia.

All these Indo-Chinese people seem to have come originally from north-western China, following the beds of great rivers in their travel ; down the Chindwin, the Irrawaddy, and the Salween into Burma, down the Brahmaputra into Assam, and up the Brahmaputra into Tibet. There seem to have been at least three waves of migration. First, in prehistoric times, there was a Mon-Khmer invasion into Further India and Assam. Next, also at an unknown date, was a Tibeto-Burman invasion into the same regions and Tibet. Next the Tai branch of the Siamese-Chinese entered eastern Burma about the sixth century A.D. A fourth Tibeto-Burmese invasion, that of the Kachins, when in Lord Dufferin's time, the British annexed Upper Burma.

I think I have now said enough to show how the

languages of India are distributed. It only remains to give a brief and cursory account of the Indian Religions. This is a subject on which big books might be, and have been, written. But, even in so small a book on the Peoples of India it seems necessary to give some account of their religious divisions.

CHAPTER III

THE RELIGIONS OF INDIA

(1) *Animism.* At the base of all the religions, perhaps at the base of all religions all over the world, lies a mass of primitive beliefs, not perhaps yet consciously classed by the holders of them as distinctly religious, which are called by the question-begging name of Animism. By this statement, I mean merely that many of the more ignorant and simple folk who profess and call themselves Hindus, Buddhists, Jains, Muhammadans, or Christians, are in fact at the animistic stage of intellectual evolution. The religious impulse is there, but has not become specialised. There is no religious theorising, but merely communal and transmitted beliefs about the nature of things in general. Perhaps I had better quote Sir H. H. Risley's definition of Hinduism as it exists in India. "It conceives of man," he says, "as

A.   6

passing through life surrounded by a ghostly company
of powers, elements, tendencies, mostly impersonal in
their character, shapeless phantasms of which no
image can be made and no definite idea can be
formed.   Some of these have departments or spheres
of influence of their own: one presides over cholera,
another over small-pox, another over cattle disease;
some dwell in rocks, others haunt trees, others, again,
are associated with rivers, whirlpools, waterfalls, or
strange pools hidden in the depths of the hills.   All
of them require to be diligently propitiated by reason
of the ills which proceed from them, and usually the
land of the village provides the means for their
propitiation."

If this definition, that of a kindly and experienced
student of primitive thought and emotion, be correct,
there is already an attempt at analysis and classification.   But the analysis is feeble, the classification
very elementary.   The differences which seem obvious
to the civilised man, who inherits the analytic inven-
tions and investigations of long series of ancestors, are
not yet realised.   There is practically no distinction
between things animate and inanimate, since all may
be maleficent and must therefore, on occasion, be
propitiated.   There is no sense of things subter-human,
human, and superhuman.   Still less, of course, is there
any recognition of the difference between things religious and things secular.   Grown men face the facts

of life as children do, and receive the impressions
life conveys to them *en masse*, without making much
effort to sort them out. In our own case, we learn
to classify from our elders, and classification, literary,
scientific, social, religious, is a large part of what we
call education. How does primitive man begin to
sort out the facts of life, to remember them in classes,
to discriminate between human beings and other
animals, to place animals above inanimate things,
himself above animals, and, finally, the gods above
himself? The history of the evolution of Hinduism
throws some light on this evolution as it occurred in
India.

Meanwhile, it is worth noticing that the Census
returns of 1901 returned the Animists of India at
only about 8½ millions, or less than 3 per cent. Those
who returned themselves as Hindu or Musalmān
were so recorded, whatever their degree of mental
and social culture. An attempt has been made in the
Census of 1911 to distinguish between true Hindus
and Animists who call themselves Hindu. How far
the attempt was successful, I do not know. I can
well believe that it was not welcomed even by
educated and intelligent Hindus. Many years ago,
I remember a highly educated Hindu in Bengal tell-
ing me that there is no distinction between Animists
and Hindus; that an Animist is merely a Hindu "in
the making" as it were. But perhaps that assertion

only amounted to an admission that the Hindu mind
is averse from the kind of intellectual evolution by
conscious analysis and classification which is dear to
Western imaginations.   Yet the history of Hinduism
and its branches shows that such an evolution has
taken place.

I should like to suggest that at the stage of
human evolution which we call animistic, man takes
the facts of life in the lump, as it were, and does not
sort them out into classes.   If we are to judge by
what we know of the history of Hinduism, the evolution of primitive man from this unclassifying stage
is something as follows.   Art comes into play.   The
practice of song and draughtsmanship introduces
specialisation.   From singing comes verse, from
drawing comes some kind of rude writing.   The first
trains the memory, the second aids memory.   Then
comes the social classification which results from the
breaking up of clans, and contact with other clans
and communities.   All men are not the same, and
the difference is grasped and finds expression in
language.   The new power of classification is extended to other things.   The difference between
animate and inanimate things is understood, and
their relative powers of helping or hurting the tribal
community.   When classification has proceeded thus
far, the inference is easy that as what is known of
the faculties of subter-human beings and things to

Plate VII

A Ghāsiya
(Mirzapur district)

benefit or hurt humans does not by any means account for the joys and calamities of life, there must be a class of superhuman beings who are to be conciliated. By their supposed deeds they are judged. If they are, on the whole, kindly and easily placated, they will be classified by some title which they will usually share with great and good men. If their action on mankind be harmful, they will bear the names given to malicious or inimical races or individuals. At a subsequent stage of analytical evolution their generic names will be confined to their own class; they will be gods or demons. Many Hindus have hardly gone beyond this stage, and we can hardly be surprised that some objection should be taken to too rigid a distinction between Hindus and Animists. In practice, it is often difficult to say whether a given observance is Animistic or Hindu. Here is one case, out of thousands that occur in India, from my own experience. In the seaport town of Chittagong is the shrine of the famous Muhammadan saint Pir Badr, a holy man often invoked by travellers on sea or river. In a niche in a little pillar in the open air, Christians and Buddhists, Hindus and Musalmāns alike place lighted candles by way of propitiation. This, surely, is an observance of the Animistic type. It has no part in any theorised or classified religious system. It is merely the attempt to gratify an influence which may help or harm.

Animism is consistent with the most vivid, if child-like, curiosity. All is grist that comes to that primitive mill. But the resulting flour of thought is, as it were, coarse and unsifted. Artistic speciali-sation, the birth of literature, brings a need of classification. Out of propitiation comes ritual, a belief in the efficacy of sacramental gestures, offer-ings, formulæ. But, as time goes on, they are appropriated to the service of highly specialised deities. As man learns the advantage of a division of labour and a specialisation of function, so his gods become "departmental." The classification will not be that of modern times. Among animate things will be reckoned fire, and air, the sun and moon and the twinkling stars. But the process of analysing and sorting will have begun.

(2) *The Vedas.* The Aryan immigrants seem to have brought a scanty and summary theology with them, or it may be that in different surroundings they forgot their old religious ideas, and, with the help of Dravidian and other aboriginal speculations, evolved new ones. Sir G. Grierson has suggested that the fact that they migrated in two afterwards hostile bodies finds its reflection, in the Vedas, in the fabled antagonism of the rival priests Visvāmitra and Vasishta; in the Mahābhāratā in the famous war between the Kauravas and Pāndavas, the Eastern counterpart of the siege of Troy.

The Vedas are four collections of ritual hymns, used in connection with the oblation of the intoxicating juice of the Soma, the moon-plant, or with the sacrificial Fire. The Rig-veda (the oldest) and its supplement the Sāma-veda are now held to have been composed when the Aryans had reached the junction of the Panjāb rivers with the Indus : the Black and White Yajur-veda when they reached the Sutlej and the Jumna; the Atharva-veda, which contains the lower beliefs of aboriginal races, when they had reached Benares. There are gods and goddesses of the sky, the most important being the Sun, and Varuna (the Greek οὐρανός), afterwards a kind of Hindu Neptune, but in these early days represented as sitting in the vault of heaven, and having the sun and stars as the eyes with which he watches the doings of men. His function was to encourage personal holiness as a human ideal. In the mid-air Indra became pre-eminent on Indian soil, where the dependence of an agricultural people on periodical rains made the rain-god an important deity. On earth the most important deities are Soma and Agni (fire) already mentioned. There was also Yama, the beautiful and stately god of death, who though naturally immortal chose to die, and lead the way for mortal successors to the abodes of the dead. Besides the departmental gods, there is in the Vedas a distinct foreshadowing of Pantheism.

(3) *The Brāhmanas.* When the Aryans reached the "Midland," the upper Gangetic valley, the Vedic hymns were supplemented by new Scriptures, called Brāhmanas, which were digests of dicta on matters of ritual for the guidance of priests. These were the beginning of Brāhmanism. The elementary Pantheistic theory of the Vedas was developed into a belief in one Spiritual Being or Ātman. When manifested and impersonal, this Being was the neuter Brahma; when regarded as the Creator, he was the masculine Brahmā; but when manifested in the highest order of intellectual men, he was Brāhman, the Brāhman priestly class. Following the Brāhmanas, was a third order of religious literature, the Upanishads. Dr Hopkins has thus summarised the teaching of these three Scriptures. "In the Vedic hymns, man fears the gods. In the Brāhmanas man subdues the gods, and fears God. In the Upanishads man ignores the gods and becomes God." Not that these three kinds of Scripture, these three evolutions of religious speculation, followed one another in chronological order. But this was, roughly, the logical evolution. Finally the doctrine was established that knowledge leads to the supreme bliss of absorption into Brahmā, and with this was combined the theory of transmigration.

Even from this extremely crude and simplified statement, it will be evident that the priesthood had secured for themselves an unexampled supremacy, and, in the Midland at least, had placed the administrator and warrior in a state of marked inferiority. But in the surrounding territories, success in arms and government won men the consideration still considered their due among ourselves. In the Midland itself the territory was divided among a number of petty chiefs, who waged perpetual warfare with one another. They were not likely to ignore the prestige won by valour and warlike skill. One of them was Gautama, the Buddha (c. 596–508 B.C.). Another was Vardhamāna, his contemporary, the founder of Jainism. This is not the place to tell of Buddhism, which, as a recognised creed, though it has spread far to the north and east, and is the religion of Ceylon and Burma, only survives in India proper in faint influences on the belief and practice of various Hindu sects.

(4) *Jainism.* The Jain Reform still exists and numbers over a million of followers. Its doctrines have a vague and general resemblance to those of Buddhism, not because either copied the other, but because they sprang from a common origin. In both Nirvāna, the "blowing out," as it were, of the lamp of life is the goal aimed at. But to the Buddhist, Nirvāna means the peace of extinction; to the Jain, it is final escape from the body after various metamorphoses. Mr Crooke defines the fivefold vow of

the Jains as prescribing (1) the sanctity of human
life; (2) renunciation of lying, which proceeds from
anger, greed, fear or mirth; (3) refusal to take things
not given; (4) chastity; (5) renunciation of worldly
attachments. The Jain pantheon consists of deified
saints who are either Tīrthan-kara, "making a passage
through the circuit of life," or Jina, "the victorious
ones."

(5) *Hinduism Proper.* These reforms, joined
with the spread of the Brāhmanical faith into lands
where the authority of Aryan priests was not recognised, produced something which, in its way, resembles
the Protestant Reformation. The Vedic religion had
come to be the monopoly of a limited order of
hereditary priests. This ritual supremacy was broken
up by two influences. A new national ideal of worship
found expression in the Epics, which to this day, in
metrical translations, are the layman's scripture all
over India.   Secondly, the Vedic pantheon was
enormously enlarged by the admission of non-Aryan
deities and aboriginal modes of worship. Hence arose
the body of writings known as the Purānas, or "ancient"
books, not all really old in the trace of their composi-
tion, but perhaps deserving their title as containing
very old beliefs. Of all these books and their teaching
other authorities have written recently in various
works on the early history and religious poetry of
India, and it would therefore be presumptuous for

me to say anything about the religious literature of Hinduism. It is sufficient to say that the Epics introduced, in place of the vague and shadowy Vedic gods, heroic incarnations of divine virtue, wisdom and valour, and thus led to the sectarian worship of the two active members of a new supreme triad of gods, Brahmā, the creator, Vishnu, the preserver, and Siva, the destroyer. Most Hindus are now followers of one or other of the two latter in some incarnation. In early times this sectarian rivalry led to wars and persecutions, but Hinduism is singularly tolerant in matters of belief and doctrine. A Saiva is not a disbeliever in the divinity of the incarnations of Vishnu ; a Vaishnava recognises the ascetic powers of Siva. But each has his favourite deity and chiefly studies the scriptures relating to him. The principal incarnations of Vishnu are Krishna and Rāma, who seem to have been originally deified heroes of the Midland. There were many Vishnuvite reformers, some of whom, it is interesting to note, may have derived suggestions from the early Christianity of Southern India.

The first of these was Rāmānuja, who lived in the eleventh century A.D. Fifth in succession to him was Rāmānanda, who lived in the fourteenth century and was the missionary of popular Vaishnavism in Northern India. To him that tract owes the prevalence of the cult of Rāma and his wife Sītā, the hero and heroine of the Epic known as the Rāmāyana. His chief

innovation was the admission of low-caste disciples
into the communion. His disciple, the famous Kabir
(1380–1420 A.D.), went further. He even linked
Hinduism with Islam. Himself a humble weaver,
he taught the spiritual equality of all men. God is
one, he argued, by whatever name men choose to call
Him. The accidents of life, social station and caste,
happiness and grief, prosperity and misfortune, are
all the results of Māya or Illusion. Happiness comes
not by formula or sacrifice but by passionate adora-
tion (*bhakti*) of God. Kabir's chief importance in
the history of Hindu evolution is in the fact that his
doctrines were the origin of Sikhism.

Another great name in the democratic Vaishnava
reformation was that of Chaitanya (1485–1527 A.D.).
Mr E. A. Gait writes of him that he was "a Baidik
Brāhman. He preached mainly in Central Bengal
and Orissa, and his doctrine found ready acceptance
among large numbers of the people, especially among
those who were still, or had only recently ceased to
be, Buddhists. This was mainly due to the fact that
he drew his followers from all sources, so much so
that even Muhammadans followed him. He preached
vehemently against the immolation of animals in
sacrifice, and the use of animal food and stimulants,
and taught that the true road to salvation lay in
bhakti, or fervent devotion to God. He recommended
Rādhā worship, and taught that the love felt by her

for Krishna was the highest form of devotion. The acceptable offerings were flowers, money, and the like ; but the great form of worship was the Sankirtan, or procession of worshippers playing and singing. The peculiarity of Chaitanya's cult is that the post of spiritual guide, or Goshain, is not confined to Brāhmans, and several of those best known belong to the Baidya caste[1]."

The Sikhs. As a religious system, the creed of the Sikhs originated from the Hindu teaching of Kabir, and may yet be reabsorbed into Hinduism, though the Census of 1911 shows that it still flourishes as a separate religion. It began as a religious reform and ended by being a political organisation. It was founded by the Guru Nānak (1469–1538 A.D.) in the Panjāb. Its formula was the Unity of God and the Brotherhood of Man. Ultimately it became a martial brotherhood, one of whose objects was by training, diet, and self-denial to present a strong front to the encroachments of Muhammadan invaders from across the north-west frontier. Circumstances led the Sikh confederacy to try its fortune in arms in two fiercely fought campaigns with the growing power of our East India Company. Defeat was followed by a loyal acceptance of British supremacy, and the Sikhs rival

---

[1] Some account of the development of Chaitanya's teaching in Assam may be found in an article of mine in Dr Hastings' *Dictionary of Religion and Ethics.*

the Gurkhas as the best soldiers in the Indian army.
Their services during the mutiny of 1857 will never
be forgotten.

The Sāktas. One other great Hindu sect, that of
the Sāktas, must be briefly mentioned. It worships
the active female principle (*prakriti*) of one or other
of the forms of the Consort of Siva—Durgā, Kāli, or
Pārvati. This cult arose in Eastern Bengal or Assam
about the fifth century, A.D., and has its own scriptures
in the Tantras. This sect is probably due to the
recrudescence of very ancient aboriginal cults. It
is associated with blood-offerings and libidinous rites.
It was denounced by the Vaishnava reformers, but
still survives, even among educated men. It affected
the later forms of Buddhism.

Finally, by omitting all mention of numerous
modern Vaishnava sects, we come to the modern
Theistic sects. The Brahmo Samāj of Bengal was
founded by the celebrated Raja Ram Mohan Roy
(1774–1833) who died and was buried at Clifton.
His teachings were continued and developed by his
successors Maharshi Devendranāth Tagore (the father
of the poet Rabindranāth Tagore), Keshav Chandra
Sen, and Pratāp Chandra Majumdār. All of these
were men of much piety, eloquence, and learning.
Sir Alfred Lyall says that "Brahmoism, as propagated
by its latest expounders, seems to be unitarianism of
a European type, and as far as one can understand

its argument, appears to have no logical stability or
locus standi between revelation and pure rationalism;
it propounds either too much or too little to its
hearers." It has, however, been an effectual bar
to the spread of Christianity among the educated
classes in Bengal. It enables them to remain in
touch with Hinduism, from which an adoption of
any European creed would effectually divide them.
Its services of praise and prayer, with a sermon or
discourse, are held on Sundays, and in form resemble
those of the Christian free churches. Its creed consists in a belief in the Unity of God, the brotherhood
of man, and direct communion with God without the
intervention of any mediator. It may fairly be
claimed for it that it has satisfied the religious needs
of men most of whom lead exemplary and in some
cases saintly lives, without compelling them to join
what is regarded as a foreign and uncongenial
religion. But for Ram Mohan Roy, educated Bengal
might well have furnished the nucleus of a Christian
Church of India, since, before his time, many distinguished and able converts were made. I need
only mention the late Rev. K. M. Bannerjee. The
Brahmo Samāj is divided into three sections. The
Ādi Samāj, as its name indicates, is the original
church. It is the most conservative of the three,
and takes its inspiration wholly from the Hindu
scriptures, and especially from the Upanishads. The

Navavidhān Samāj, founded by Keshav Chandra Sen, "the Church of the New Dispensation," is much more eclectic and has borrowed what it considers acceptable, not only from the holy books of Hinduism, but from Christianity, Buddhism, and Islam. The Sādhāran (or "general") Brāhmo Samāj is the most advanced of the three Churches. It rejects caste and the seclusion of women, allows inter-caste marriages, and is seemingly as far from orthodox Hinduism as from orthodox Christianity. It has even allowed one of its lady members to be married to an Englishman by Brāhmo rites. If it can hardly be called Hindu in ritual or in belief, it is Hindu in what is probably regarded as the more important sense of being a purely Indian sect and not a direct product of European missionary zeal.

Another new sect, the Ārya Samāj, or Aryan Society, has much influence in the Panjāb and North-Western India generally. It was founded by Dayānand Saraswati (1827–53). Its only scriptures are the Vedas. It professes pure monotheism, repudiates idol worship, and is much interested in social reform. It has also at times been mixed up, more or less directly, with political agitation. Like the Brāhmo Samāj, it is probably due in its inception to the influence of European religious teaching, but, as is perhaps natural, its acceptance of European ethics is marked by a sturdy resistance to European dogma.

The great bulk of Hinduism, however, remains still but little removed from the Animistic stage of religious evolution, and one of the results of the spread of British rule into wild and savage tracts has been the extension of the borders of Hinduism in competition with Christianity.   In the rougher and wilder races, not yet sufficiently softened and civilised for the acceptance of the Hindu social system, the Christian missionary prevails.   He has been most successful among the Gonds of Central India, among such savage tribes as the Nāgas, Gāros, and Lushais on the Assam border.   Elsewhere Hinduism pursues its quietly imperturbable course and admits savage races to its lower castes as it has always admitted them during the last two thousand years.

Islam in India.   Since King George V has more Muhammadan subjects than any other ruler on earth—some 75,000,000 in number, it would not be proper to close a little book on the Peoples of India without saying something of those of their number who are Musalmāns.   The early Muhammadan invasions of the tenth century were mere predatory raids, and were attended neither by settlement nor conversion.   But at the end of the twelfth century Muhammad Ghori overthrew the Hindu dynasties of Delhi and Kanauj and thus opened the way to future Muhammadan conquests.   In the sixteenth

century Moghal rule was established under Babar
and his successors. During the preceding five
centuries Hindu India suffered much oppression
and wrong at the hands of Muhammadan invaders,
but Islam had made no attempt to become an
Indian religion. The early Moghal emperors were
too busy in consolidating their conquests and organ-
ising their administration to have much leisure or
inclination, for proselytising. Their policy depended
largely on co-operation with Rājput princes, whose
daughters they married. The influence of Rājput
empresses and princesses made for kindly tolerance.
It was only under the zealot Aurangzeb that any
tendency to forcible conversion showed itself.

The final result of some seven hundred years of
Muhammadan rule in various parts of the country is
that Musalmāns are in excess of Hindus only in the
Western Panjāb, which is in contact with a purely
Muhammadan country, and in Eastern Bengal, where
the aboriginal low-caste Hindu was glad to get social
promotion by accepting Islam, and where he thrives
and prospers at the expense of his Hindu brother,
partly because his diet is more nutritious, partly
because he does not practise infant-marriage and
other debilitating customs.

As has been said above, Animism has affected
Islam as well as Hinduism. From the old religion of
the country Musalmāns have borrowed demonology,

a belief in witchcraft, and the worship of departed
Pirs or saints. The most remarkable instance of the
latter is the sect of the Pachpiriyas of Bengal, the
worshippers of the Five Saints, a cult which some
have traced to the cult of the five Pāndava heroes of
the Mahābhārata. The five Pirs, however, vary in
name from district to district. In Eastern Bengal,
no one, whether Hindu or Musalmān (or, I had
almost said, Christian), begins a journey by boat
without a loud and hearty invocation of the Ganges,
the Wind, the Five Pirs, and Pir Badr before
mentioned.

Of the two great sects of Islam, the Sunnis and
the Shias, the former are by far the most numerous
in India. The Sunnis or Traditionalists accept the
Sunnat or collected body of Arabic usage as possessing authority concurrent with that of the Koran,
which is the sole scripture of the Shias. Yet in
Eastern Bengal the annual procession of the Tazias,
or representations of the tombs of the martyred
grandsons of the Prophet, is much attended by
Sunnis (though for them the practice is unortho-
dox), and indeed by Hindus also. In other parts
of India, the Mohurram festival has often led to
serious encounters between Hindus and Musalmāns,
and even in Calcutta and Bombay has been the
cause of dangerous riots.

The sects of Islam in India, unlike the Hindu

sects, are not due to the instinct for differentiation, for obvious reasons. They are, in Mr Crooke's words, either puritanical or pietistic. Consequently, followers of them are apt to show a tendency to fanaticism. The Hindu sectarian adores some favourite deity, but does not deny the merits, or the Hinduism, of other deities or their followers. The Musalmān sectarian is one who has discovered a higher orthodoxy than others, or a straighter road to religion, and regards those who do not share his views as an enemy of God and the true faith. Of the puritanical sects, the best known is that of the Wahābis, founded by Ibn Abdul Wahāb at Nejd in Arabia, at the beginning of the eighteenth century. It was an attempt to revive primitive Muhammadanship without the corruptions and accretions of later ages and foreign lands. It was brought into India by Sayid Ahmad Shāh, who proclaimed a Jihād, or holy war, against the Sikhs in 1826. The Wahābis hold that the doctrine of the Unity of God has been endangered by the excessive reverence paid to the Prophet, to his successors the Imāns, and to shrines. At times Wahābis have given trouble to the administration, especially in Bengal. In recent years, however, they call themselves Ahl-i-hadīs, or "followers of tradition," and employ themselves chiefly in endeavouring to eradicate modern superstitions.

The pietistic sects tend towards Sūfi-ism, a

combination of Aryan pantheism with Semitic monotheism, which takes the form of ecstatic devotion.
Something of the same kind may be found in the
Vaisnav sects of Hinduism, and in both cases ultimate
absorption in the divinity is the goal aimed at.

Very interesting local communities of Muhammadans are the Moplahs of the Malabar coast,
descendants of Arab settlers; the Bohras or
"traders" of Western India; and the Khojās, followers of the "Old Man of the Mountain," whose
present representative is H.H. the Agha Khān of
Bombay, who has many friends in England.

The Pārsīs. The word Pārsī simply means Persian,
and the Pārsī religion is the dualistic faith, combined
with fire-worship, of the ancient Persians.   It is also
called Mazdaism from Ahura Mazda (Ormuzd), who
is in perpetual conflict with Angro Mainyush (Ahri-
man), the spirit of evil.   It is also called Zoroastrian-
ism, from the reformer Zoroaster, the Greek form of
the old Iranian Zarathushtra, the modern Persian
Zardusht.   The religious phraseology of the Pārsīs
shows that their faith must have had a common
origin with the Aryan religion of India before the
Iranian and Indo-Aryan migrations parted company.
By a curious trick of language, the Devas, who in
India and Europe are beneficent gods, in Persia
become evil spirits.   In India by a corresponding
inversion, the word Asura, which in the Rig-veda

is still a name of gods, was applied to hostile (gene-rally aboriginal) demons. By a further process Asura was regarded as a negative word, and gave birth to a tribe of beneficent Suras. In the earlier times, there were both Ahura and Daeva worshippers, the former being socially superior, cattle-breeders, who, like the Indian Hindus, venerated the cow. It was Zoroaster's mission to fuse these two cults into a dualistic creed, whose main principle was the continuous struggle between the powers of good and evil. Submerged for a time during the Greek occupation, the Mazdaist faith revived under the Sassanids, but was finally overthrown by the advent of Islam, which persecuted and strove to extirpate the worship of fire.

Many of the survivors migrated to India, where they secured the tolerance of Hindu and Muhammadan rulers alike, and increased and multiplied. Up to the middle of the eighteenth century, Surat, Nausāri, and the neighbouring parts of Gujarāt were their home. When, under British rule, Bombay became a great commercial port, large numbers of Pārsīs migrated thither, and in many cases won great wealth and influence.

In the early days of their dispersion, the weak colonies of Pārsīs assimilated themselves with the lower classes of Hindus by whom they were sur-rounded. But fresh accessions from Irān, and a growth of national prosperity and self-confidence brought about a restoration of the ancient faith. On Indian soil, the Pārsīs now number 94,000. But owing to their intelligence and wealth, due to their remarkable success in trading, the Pārsīs command a much wider political and social influence than their numbers would seem to show. According to Pārsī belief, the soul passes after death to paradise (Bihisht) or a place of punishment (Dozakh) according to a man's conduct in life. Much importance is attached to the performance of rites to the *manes* of ancestors. Fire, water, the sun, moon, and stars were created by Ahura Mazda, and are venerated, as is Zarathushtra the Prophet. Soshios, his son, will some day be reincarnated as a Messiah, and will convert the world to the true faith. As with other Indian religions, contact with Europeans tends to produce laxity of belief and conduct.

Christianity. It is interesting to remember that there were Christians in India before the Christian faith reached our islands. The tradition that St Thomas was the Apostle of India, and suffered martyrdom there, is indeed discredited. This tradition originated with the Syriac *Acta Thomae*, and was accepted by Catholic teachers from the middle of the fourth century. The Indian King Gundaphar of the *Acta* is undoubtedly the historical Gondophares, whose dynasty was Parthian, though his territories were loosely considered to extend to India. A full account of the traditions connecting St Thomas with India (by W. R. Philipps) will be found in vol. XXXII. of the *Indian Antiquary*, 1903, pp. 1–15, 145–160.

The term "Christians of St Thomas" is often applied to the members of the ancient Christian churches of Southern India which claim him as their first founder, and honour as their second founder a bishop called Thomas, who is said to have come from Jerusalem to Malabar in 345 A.D. According to local tradition, St Thomas went from Malabar to Mylapur, now a suburb of Madras and the seat of a Roman Catholic bishop. Here still exists the shrine of his martyrdom on Mount St Thomas. A miraculous cross is shown with a Pahlavi inscription which is said to be as old as the end of the seventh century. The old churches of the south were certainly of East Syrian origin. They never wholly lost their sense of connection with their mother church, for it is known that they sent deputies in 1490 to the Nestorian patriarch Simeon, who provided them with bishops. Under Musalmān rule, they suffered severely, and welcomed the advent of the Portuguese to India. They were, however, recalcitrant to Roman influence, and it was with much difficulty that in 1599 they were induced to submit to a formal union with Rome at the synod of Diamper (Udayamperur in Cochin). During the following century and a half the Thomasine churches were under foreign Jesuit rule, but yielded an unwilling and intermittent obedience. In 1653, there was a great schism, and of about 200,000 Christians of St Thomas only 400 remained loyal to Rome, though some of their churches were soon won back by the Carmelites. The remainder fell under the influence of the Jacobite Mar Gregorius, styled patriarch of Jerusalem, who reached Malabar in 1665 as an emissary from Ignatius patriarch of Antioch. From this time, the independent churches of Southern India have been Jacobite. At the present time, they are on friendly terms with the Anglican church in India, and are loosening their dependence on the Jacobite patriarch of Antioch.

Of missionary work in India I need not speak in a book of this size. There are nearly three millions of Christians in India, of whom two and a half millions are native converts. Seeing that missionary work has been in operation since 1500, a tale of converts amounting to less than one per cent. may seem a discouraging result of over 400 years of contact with European religious thought. But actual conversion has taken place chiefly among the lower classes and least advanced races. Among the educated classes the influence of Christianity has been indirect, and in many cases has produced a transformation in ethical belief and social conduct as complete as could have been wrought by open conversion. The Brāhmo Samāj, for instance, remains Hindu in a sense, because it refuses to sever its connection with India, or to acknowledge European authority in matters of religion. But the Brāhmo Samāj could not have come into existence but for Rām Mohan Roy's friendly and intimate acquaintance with European Christians and Unitarians. Even in the matter of conversion, the rate of progress is increasing rapidly, partly because missionary effort is being directed to savage tracts hitherto unvisited by civilised men, but partly, also, because the native Christian community is beginning to have sufficient self-confidence and status to proselytise in its turn. The multiplicity of missionary agencies, due to the accidents of European history and development, has been an impediment. Such terms as the Church of England, Church of Scotland, Welsh Baptists, American Baptists, etc., can have little signification for races who cannot be expected to know the historical causes which brought about these local varieties of Christian doctrine and practice. There may yet arise among one of the rival churches in India a Christian Rāmanuja or Chaitanya, who may found a great Church of India, with a ritual, and, perhaps, doctrines of its own. The most successful of the Jesuit missionaries, Robert de Nobili[1] for instance, and such men as the Abbé Dubois in

[1] In 1606, R. de Nobili, a nephew of Bellarmine, was in charge of the Jesuit mission at Madura, and adopted the costume of a Dravidian Brāhman.

later times, owed their success to the fact that they assumed the habits, dress, and often the titles of Brāhmanic ascetics.   They could not assume the dusky skin which, after all, is the first and easiest means of gaining an Indian's confidence.   They could not wholly accept caste, they could not wink at polygamy in the case of men whose first wives were infertile, and who had an hereditary sense that the lack of an heir is socially and religiously reprehensible.   Perhaps a truly indigenous Church of India may deal with such difficulties more successfully than men who are compelled to teach, not only the elements of the Christian faith, but the ethical traditions belonging to their own race.

In this connection, I may be allowed to conclude my necessarily brief story of Indian races and religions with an anecdote.   Just thirty-five years ago I was in charge of a "subdivision" in Bengal which contained a large number of native Christians belonging to the Church of England.   There were several churches with parsonages, and the nearest of these to my headquarters was in the charge of a young missionary who was glad to have an occasional chat with a young magistrate.   One day my missionary friend told me that he had discovered with dismay that his flock were in the habit of attending the Communion Service in batches, according to their castes, so as not to be obliged to drink out of the cup with men of alien caste.

There were Hindu Christians and Muhammadan
Christians who could not eat or drink together. He
decided that this state of things must be stopped at
all costs, as being wholly contrary to Christian teaching. I ventured to suggest that spiritual equality is
not the same thing as social equality, but had to
admit that caste is not usually recognised as a Christian institution. Apparently the Christians listened
to their pastor's admonition, for, a few days after, he
rode over to say that, in consequence of ex-scavengers
and ex-Brāhmans having communicated together, his
whole congregation had been put out of caste by their
Hindu neighbours. This may not, at first sight, seem
a very serious calamity. But it happened that, in the
caste specialisation which had survived among the
Christians, there were none of the community who
were barbers or midwives by caste. Christian men
were going about with stubbly chins : worse still,
Christian women were in need of help which their
Hindu sisters refused to supply. It was a difficult
situation for two young bachelors. However, I
now confess, after all these years, that I brought a
little official pressure to bear on the midwives, and
the situation was saved for the moment. In those
days, the educational policy of Government was to
give grants-in-aid to primary schools, most of which,
in this very Christian "sub-division" were either
Roman Catholic or Anglican. When next I proceeded

to issue my doles according to school-population and
other educational results, I was astonished to find
that the Roman Catholic grant-in-aid had increased
greatly and the Anglican grant-in-aid had propor-
tionally diminished. This was the immediate (and no
doubt temporary) result of my missionary friend's
zeal. Such survivals of old beliefs are common in all
the religions of India. The main social impulse of
the people was implanted on their minds at the distant
epoch of the Aryan settlement, the sense of social and
racial inequality which has now hardened into the
caste system. To most Indians a recognition of the
importance and value of caste is the first step towards
decent and seemly conduct, towards civilised morality.
When a semi-savage hill-man begins to recognise his
inferiority to his Hindu neighbours and makes tenta-
tive approaches with a view to inclusion in civilised
society, his first duty is to abjure the diet of pork
and rice-beer which his unregenerate appetite loves,
since these indulgences stand in the way of sharing
a meal with Hindu folk. (In other parts of India,
liquor and meat are consumed by low-caste Hindus
of aboriginal origin.) In Assam, a Kachāri first
accepts the *sarana* or "protection" of a Hindu
Goshain. He is then called a Saraniya Koch. His
next step is to abandon strong drinks, on which he is
promoted to the status of a Modāhi Koch. At this
stage, he may be fortunate enough to win the hand

of a bride of pure Koch family, and, under her guidance, acquires enough of conventional habits and beliefs to be recognised as a Kāmtāli or Bor Koch, and is a true Hindu, a member of a genuine Hindu caste. Musalmāns and Christians have other social conventions, and do not usually regard them as essential to good manners or godliness. But their converts retain their social superstitions and carry them into the new surroundings, where they sometimes come into disagreeable contact with the ethical ideas belonging to imported religions.

The contact of Aryan with Dravidian races, some three thousand years ago, brought about the beginnings of caste, which, from one point of view, may be regarded as a rude form of "race-protection," a primitive system of eugenics. It is still most rigidly enforced in the south, where the semi-Aryan classes are in a great minority. It is most relaxed in the Panjāb, where, though caste rules exist, the population is, and probably always has been, as homogeneous as our own race. French travellers in India have sometimes said, half-humorously, that the Anglo-Indian administrators and merchants are practically a caste unto themselves. Bengalis have made the same remark and have said that our Civil Service is composed of *Kali Yuger Brāhman*, "the Brāhmans of the Iron Age." There was once some truth in the accusation, if accusation it be. It was not our business to interfere deliberately with caste, since British policy from the first has been one of kindly neutrality and toleration. Whether indirect influences have mitigated the effect of the sentiment of caste is a moot point. Educated Indians who have lived in Europe see its irksomeness, and in some cases denounce it more vigorously than most Europeans will care to denounce a system due to historical causes which are still partly operative. On the other hand, railways and other facilities for travel, though they have necessarily introduced laxity in matters of food and contact, have probably heightened the caste feeling by emphasising the variety of Hindu humanity and of the customs and habits of its many races. Hence the evolution of Indian society remains as interesting and as incalculable as ever.

In a little book of this sort it has been necessary to make many general and sweeping statements which are not always literally true of any given part of India. But perhaps enough has been said to show the interesting and significant differences between the three hundred odd millions of Western Europe and the three hundred odd millions of India. Our business in India has been primarily to keep the peace, to provide a breathing-space after the social and political turmoil that followed on the breaking-up of the Moghal empire. The principal result, so far, has been a notable increase in Hindu self-confidence and ambition, and a growing belief among Hindus that their ancient social system is not incompatible with industrial, commercial, and political advance on European lines. This belief has been much strengthened by the modernisation of Japan, and its results. It has been fostered by the free admission of educated Hindus to the highest and most responsible posts in the King-Emperor's administration. Inasmuch as that statement brings me to the most modern development of Hindu life and thought, I cannot do better than end at this point.

BIBLIOGRAPHY

CHAPTER I

The standard authority on the Hindu literary theory of Caste is M. Emile Senart's *Les Castes dans l'Inde*. Paris. Ernest Leroux. 1896.

Probably the best succinct account of Caste is Mr E. A. Gait's article in Dr Hastings' *Encyclopædia of Religion and Ethics*. This will, of course, be brought up to date in the forthcoming Report on the Indian Census of 1911.

Sir A. C. Lyall's *Asiatic Studies*. London. John Murray. Contains a sympathetic and learned account of Hindu social life and of the workings of Caste in Upper India.

M. C. Bouglé's *Essai sur le Régime des Castes*. Paris. Felix Alcan. 1908. Contains much interesting matter taken from many sources, but sometimes, from want of local knowledge, does not sufficiently discriminate between different developments of the caste system.

There is an enormous literature on the races, tribes, and castes of India, but references to the most important books will be found in the above authorities.

Chapter I is, in the main, a summary of Sir H. H. Risley's views as expressed in Chapter VI of Vol. I of the *Imperial Gazetteer*. That is inevitable, since the *Gazetteer* contains necessarily the most authoritative summary of what is known on the subject, pending the appearance of Mr Gait's forthcoming Census Report.

A.   8

CHAPTER II

The standard authority on the modern languages of India is Sir G. A. Grierson's work on *The Languages of India* (Calcutta, 1903). It will, however, be superseded by the book which Sir G. A. Grierson is now writing on the basis of the further materials collected in his *Linguistic Survey*, and in the Census Reports of 1911. The eleven volumes hitherto published of the *Survey* itself give specimens of the Indian languages and skeleton grammars.

CHAPTER III

Professor Macdonell's *History of Sanskrit Literature* (Heinemann, 1905) contains a fascinating and readable account of the Hindu scriptures from the Vedic ages up to modern times.

Professor Hopkins' *Religions of India* and *India Old and New* deal with both the literature and the actual working of Indian religions. Mr W. Crooke's *Native Races of Northern India* is a popular account of the Aryan region, and Mr Thurston's *Castes and Tribes of Southern India*. Madras, Government Press. 1908. Though it is more elaborate and scientific in its treatment, is full of matters which are interesting not only to the specialist.

Meredith Townsend's *Asia and Europe*. London. Archibald Constable. 1905. Is still an interesting and suggestive study of the differences between East and West, and Sir A. C. Lyall's *Asiatic Studies* are the even more illuminating results of a long, intimate, and sympathetic familiarity with Indian religious thought.

The chapter on Religion in the forthcoming Census Report for 1911 will contain the latest fruits of research, statistical and other.

There is an enormous mass of literature dealing in detail with the religions and sects of India. A selected list of books will be found at p. 446 of the *Imperial Gazetteer*.

INDEX

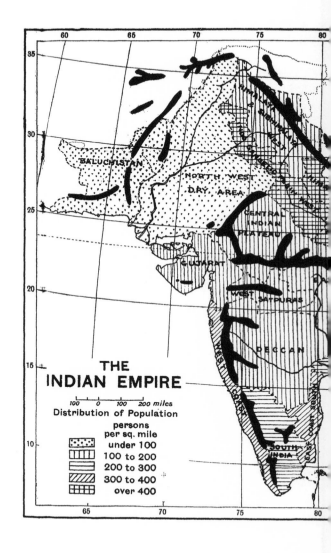

THE
INDIAN EMPIRE

100   0   100   200 miles

Distribution of Population

persons
per sq. mile
under 100
100 to 200
200 to 300
300 to 400
over 400

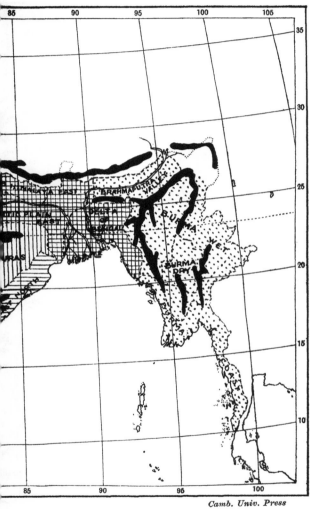

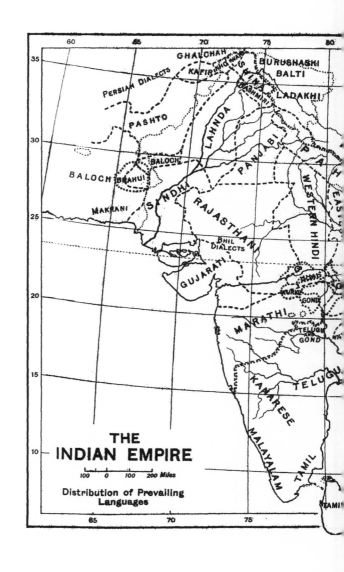

THE
INDIAN EMPIRE

100   0   100   200 Miles

Distribution of Prevailing
Languages

www.ingramcontent.com/pod-product-compliance
Ingram Content Group UK Ltd.
Pitfield, Milton Keynes, MK11 3LW, UK
UKHW042146280225
455719UK00001B/132